To Lauman
Happy Birthday
5th August 1988.
Love Willi xxx

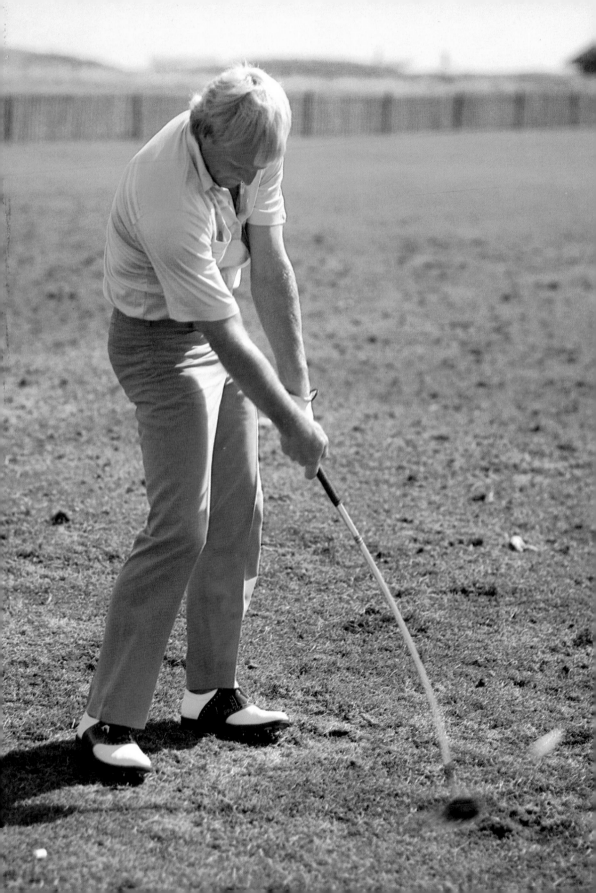

GOLF
THE
PROFESSIONAL
APPROACH

Bernard Cooke

Foreword by
Malcolm Campbell,
Editor of Golf Monthly

DEDICATED
TO THE MEMORY OF
IRVIN E. SCHLOSS

Acknowledgments

I am grateful to the Professional Golfers' Association of America for their kind assistance, to *Golf Monthly* for the use of the Hubie Smith lecture and to Richard Widdows for his valuable editorial contribution.

All photographs supplied by Bernard Cooke except for the following: Henry Cotton 45 left, 55 left; Irvin E. Schloss 7, 14, 40 left, 45 right, 55 right.

Frontispiece: Greg Norman

Published by The Hamlyn Publishing Group Limited
Bridge House, 69 London Road,
Twickenham, Middlesex TW1 3SB, England.
and distributed for them by
Octopus Distribution Services Limited
Rushden, Northamptonshire, England.

First published in 1987
Second impression 1987

ISBN 0 600 33344 2

Printed in Spain

CONTENTS

FOREWORD

At the 1986 Open Championship at Turnberry I was entertaining Henry
Cotton in the relative comfort of the *Golf Monthly* caravan when Bernard
Cooke and his wife Audrey paid us a visit. It was an interesting meeting, for
both 'The Maestro' and Bernard have been valued contributors to the
magazine for many years.

They had met only on a few occasions before that day. Bernard recalled
the only time they actually played together, during a qualifying round for
the Open Championship; if my memory serves me right it was at Birkdale
in 1961. Never had he enjoyed such a pleasant and helpful playing
companion – but while Cotton qualified, Bernard missed out by a single
stroke for the main event.

It is perhaps sad that their diverse golfing careers have not converged
more often, for I know of no two professional players who have more to
contribute in terms of imparting their knowledge of how to play the game
than these gentlemen.

While their views on the best method by which to teach the golfing
'masses' might not coincide in every respect, they emphatically agree that
there's no single way to play or to teach.

This is Bernard's second book, the follow-up to the very successful
Newnes All-Colour Guide to Golf. His unique collection of films of the top
players, supplemented by his own photographic record and studiously put
together over many years, is unrivalled anywhere in the world.

His pioneering 'freeze-frame' techniques have been invaluable in
enabling him to find the common factors that have made the great players
great and the best amateurs as good as they have become. In his ability to
interpret this material and communicate the knowledge gained from it to
the golfing world, Bernard has already made a notable contribution to the
game he loves.

I'm honoured that he has asked me to write the foreword to this very
refreshing book. I commend it in the firm belief that if the secret to being
able to play well this most frustrating of games is ever going to be found
then Bernard Cooke, with his diligence, wealth of experience and splendid
collection of reference material, is perhaps the man who is going to be
closest to finding it.

Malcolm Campbell

CHAPTER ONE

TEACHERS AND STUDENTS

Whether you're a budding professional, a skilled amateur, a handicap player or a nervous beginner, you may well be one of those golfers who avidly read books and magazines on the subject, scouring their pages with the intention of finding the hidden secret to the great golf swing. In the following chapters, I shall explore every aspect of my knowledge and experience in a quest to help you unearth that sporting elixir.

The better teaching professionals are kept busy not only by their regular disciples but also by a human caravan of golf's walking wounded, seeking the physician who can heal their ailing swings. If one teacher fails them, many will go on to the next in a desperate search for their golfing guru.

And many of you, experienced as well as novice, come to grief when you solicit the views of your golfing acquaintances; or when your well-meaning golfing friends, in all good faith, volunteer advice which all too often only deepens the existing wounds.

The late Irvin E. Schloss, to whom this book is dedicated, using his famous custom-made chair to inspect the swing of Jo-Anne Whittaker, the Florida psychiatrist who runs her own golfing workshops using 'the neurolinguistic approach'. I now use this chair myself, since it was constructed to give the ideal height from which to analyse the average swing.

Throughout this book I'll be writing, primarily as a teacher, about the best players and how they play, because that's how I teach – *the way the best players play*. I'll also be referring to, and using photographs of, some other players, both professional and amateur, and although they are by no means famous, they too have impressed me with their play and added to my knowledge of the game.

I'll be writing about teachers, and how and what they teach; and about students, and how they should learn. I will tell you all I know about the swing – its physics, its psychology, even its philosophy. And all with the intention of discovering and disclosing the panacea. The 'professional approach' serves the pros very well: I hope it can do the same for you.

Separating method from style

I've often thought how difficult it is for a player requiring help to find the right teacher, since there really are no two teachers who would spread their doctrines in precisely the same way. Just as the star players differ in style, so do the coaches vary in their teaching techniques.

Yet the message should not be confused with the medium. There has for some years now been an attempt by the professional organizations to standardize golf teaching, and the PGAs of the United States, Britain, Sweden, West Germany and Australia are among those who train their junior members to teach a basic swing method. This has the admirable objective of 'passing out' professionals who all teach the same essential thing, the idea being that you get the same fundamental approach from a teacher in Texas as you would at Turnberry. Unfortunately, in my view at least, you cannot produce such uniformity. It's like two artists with the same model, two photographers with the same subject, two conductors with the same piece of music; the results will always be different. Each teacher like each superstar has his own distinctive style.

If you analyse swings closely, however – as I've been able to do with my pioneering cinematic techniques – you'll find that in one sense they are all employing the same method. They all obey certain physical laws and share the same common 'swing factors'. And it's these factors that we will be studying in our hunt for improvement.

The art of teaching

So how does the student choose a teacher? Well, the reputation of a teacher attracts pupils, of course, and the more successful a coach is the more he can charge for his services. But it's not a simple question of 'you get what you pay for', since in any profession or trade there will always be a minority who put their wallets before their integrity. Indeed I'd say there were two basic types of golfing teacher: the concerned, 'artistic' one who really cares about his pupils, and the one who sees it at best as a living, at worst as a tiresome chore expected of a club professional. The expectant pupil should also be aware of the trap of thinking that the more he is charged, the better the tuition is bound to be.

A good teacher is usually objective rather than subjective – that is, he teaches *how to play*, not *how he plays*. The art of teaching is communicating, having the ability to see one move that will at the same time cure two or even more faults, the ability to analyse the whole golf swing completely, and knowing intimately all its component parts. It also helps to be something of a psychiatrist and a philosopher.

For many reasons, which I shall deal with elsewhere in this book, teachers are rarely outstanding players. It is doubtful if you have heard of Stewart Maiden, for example. He taught Bobby Jones, whose playing achievements from the mid-1920s to the early 1930s have not been equalled since. Come to think of it, who taught Paganini to play the violin? And who was Einstein's maths teacher? They must have been very good teachers, even though they had brilliant pupils. Teachers rarely make the limelight, but their best students could.

Very often, students are attracted to a teacher because his magazine articles, and in some cases his books, appeal to them; and it is crucially important to be on the same wavelength as your teacher from the start. I went to a number of professionals before I found Irv Schloss through his articles in *Golf Monthly* magazine. They immediately made sense to me, and after studying his method for some time I found more and more depth of truth in it. Frankly, I am still even now gleaning a wealth of golfing knowledge from his mechanics and philosophy.

When you do find the teacher from whom you feel you can learn, stick to him or her through thick and thin. He or she could be a fountain of information.

There are dozens of minor differences of views between golf teachers. I came across one of these men when I was professional to the Whitley Bay Golf Club in the north-east of England over 25 years ago. One of my colleagues taught, 'not holding with the last three left-hand fingers at all'. A few miles away, I taught (and still do), 'varying pressures from light to firm, but never loose', on those last three left-hand fingers. In this particular instance the difference was irreconcilable. I couldn't see the logic of loose left-hand fingers, but it was part of my neighbour's regular teaching pattern.

I have often been confronted with differences between my views and those of other teachers, and I can only say that where there are differences of opinion there can be good reasons for them. It may be that the student showed a weakness on a particular occasion and was needing this sort of advice to correct it, even though it did seem to conflict with the conventional approach. When the differences cannot be reconciled, I can only suggest that one of the teachers is being subjective; he may find that a particular idea suits his own game so well that he's convinced it would be as successful for all his students.

Teachers and players

Some skilled players who occasionally teach do tend to be subjective and pass on to students their own playing methods – or at least what they feel is their playing method. This isn't to say that among the highly skilled players there are no good teachers: Lee Trevino, Jack Nicklaus, Tom Watson or David Graham could hold my attention as long as they talked about the golf swing, and I believe that Greg Norman, a compulsive teacher, really knows his stuff. I took the photographs of him on page 11 when he was pointing out to Andy Bean that the American's right leg was straightening on the backswing, instead of remaining flexed in to support his centre.

But a teaching professional evolves. He will start his career tilting at the tournaments and more than likely will finance himself from the proceeds of the lessons he gives at his club. He will find himself teaching more and more if he is good, i.e. he gets results, and then the demands on his time will mean he practises less and less. When this demand for his teaching services becomes excessive (and participation in the tournament unprofitable), so will he play in fewer tournaments and spend more hours on the teaching fairway. Now he will be enjoying the successes of his students.

Eventually he will quit the tournaments and for the rest of his working life teaching will be his speciality. Playing will be more of a 'local' nature, and often something of a luxury.

The more lessons he has given the better he will tend to be. Irv Schloss, who was a top American coach, always said, 'You've got to have given over a thousand lessons before you know what you're talking about as a teacher. You should really give your early victims their money back!'

I would agree with Irv Schloss about this, but he did say it jocularly and with some reservation. Only on half a dozen occasions have I refused to take a pupil's fee, convinced that my advice was falling on stony ground. I once took on a beginner who threw out a challenge that he would pay me double my fee if I could make him play golf in one lesson, with nothing if I failed. Well, I fell for it, and after three hours I conceded: I've long ceased to teach for nothing or to take on such wagers.

The art of learning

What's required of you as a student? You must, of course, learn how to

The golfing fraternity: Greg Norman, a compulsive 'teacher', points out Andy Bean's tendency to let his right knee 'sag out' on the backswing, instead of remaining flexed in to support his centre, thus causing a faulty sway. Apparently Bean had been unaware of the problem until the Australian picked it up and the lesson, a quite spontaneous affair on the practice area, was no doubt a very helpful one. Not all top pros are good teachers, of course – any more than good teaching pros are all leading tournament players.

Most top professionals place enormous emphasis on coaching, and feel they can always learn something new to improve their game. Here Tom Kite comes under the eagle eye of leading American expert Peter Kostis, a man Kite regularly consults for advice and help. Too often the average club player regards coaching as unnecessary or taking some kind of unfair advantage, without realizing the enormous benefits it can bring to his limited game.

learn, but often the student is not a good learner. The art of learning, to put it very simply and briefly, is *listening, looking, imitating* and *asking questions* – hundreds of them.

John Pennock, a student of mine from one of my first evening classes, was and still is a great listener and a great 'looker'. He listened, he looked, he imitated and he questioned. In due course he achieved a six handicap and now, at the age of 66, his action is still machine-like, and he strikes the ball as accurately and as ever, every time.

When John went to watch his first pro tournament he asked me what I thought he should look for in the players' swings. I said, 'Try to pick out one factor common to all of them.' When I saw him later I asked him if he had found that one factor. 'Yes I have,' he replied. 'They were all completely fluid through impact to the end of the swing.' From his own powers of observation he taught me the meaning of 'continuity'. A good pupil can often help to make a good teacher.

Consistent success is the outcome of an obsessive application of a set of simple principles over an extended period of time until it becomes habitual. This is the only way to immunize yourself against cowboy coaching and phoney tips from flattering friends, those eternal stumbling blocks to a player's progress.

Help and hindrance

As a golfer being coached, avoid like the plague those would-be teachers among your playing partners, who point out that you have a right-hand palm grip instead of a finger grip when your coach is currently trying to get you to swing on a more upright plane. Such diversions are sometimes tempting because they can contain smatterings of truth, but discipline yourself to ignore them. It will not be easy, but it's better than having muddy footprints soil the picture your mentor is helping you to paint.

There's another devil, although he won't see himself as such, lurking to trap the unwary student. He will in fact believe he's your saviour when he advises you to change your coach, especially if you are suffering a sticky patch or you have reached a boring plateau. He knows 'the very one' who will solve your problems in a trice. 'He'll put you right in no time,' he says. 'Uses a totally different method from your chap.' Remember – stick to your coach through thick and thin if you're convinced he's the one for you.

Differences in method between teachers are really major gaps which no student should attempt to straddle. I will enlarge on method difference later in this book.

The temptation of 'quick and easy' methods

I can't remember who it was who once told me that some young Americans with golfing potential will adopt a formula they know will work and practise this even beyond the pain barrier. They will reduce that formula to its simplest common multiple to make it easier to remember and therefore easier to translate into a whole movement.

I can substantiate this. I've met such a type – a young American who by profession was a 'funeral salesman', who adhered to just such a formula. He had reduced his swing to virtually just 'back and through'. He could perform this with astonishing agility and strength. But it must be realized that his formula reduction was the result of habitualizing so much detail over the months and years that he was left only with having those two moves to make the ball fly far and straight. His impact explosion had the viciousness of a rifle shot.

However, you have to start at the beginning. The last coat of varnish will make a new driver look perfect, but there has to be a lot of work and craftsmanship before that final gloss is applied.

Let's move on and see what's needed to attain this 'ultimate' objective. A detailed look at my method, 'The Forward Drive', will present one way to this goal, but there are acceptable variations and alternatives, as you will see in the following pages.

I'm pretty sure you will not come across any teacher who preaches the gospel exactly as I do. But there must be a number of teachers who now teach exactly the same method who are also objective with a sprinkling of pragmatism and are non-polemic. I'm not too happy about the gimmick teachers, whose end result is more like a patchwork quilt than a silken cloak.

In the early days I was a bit of a loner in Britain with my 'American' teaching methods. But I discovered this only after enjoying several years of what I might immodestly call successful results.

I knew, implicitly and explicitly, that having seen a pupil hit a number of shots with different clubs I could change the movement so that the student would, if not immediately (and it sometimes was immediately) improve on his or her shotmaking.

Irv used to say, 'Teaching is an art and playing is a skill.' Certainly I have often wished I could have had the same confidence playing on the golf course as I had when teaching on the practice ground.

Keeping your cool

Keeping a cool head and having infinite patience is vital for teaching. If you can't keep a cool head and have the same patience for playing you're never going to achieve the levels of which you may be physically capable.

This was amply demonstrated during the final of the Suntory World Matchplay at Wentworth in 1986. Greg Norman beat Sandy Lyle in the final with some ease, but afterwards he blew up about what he saw as disgraceful and distracting partisan behaviour in the crowds. Yet during his excellent two rounds he appeared to be well in command of himself, playing controlled golf.

The inimitable Ben Hogan about to drive: perfectly poised, totally in command, and not the least perturbed by his own shadow. You can sense that he's going to make a fine shot.

Ben Hogan was the paragon of golfing patience. I never saw him playing in the flesh, although I did see him at Ganton in 1949 when he was the non-playing captain of the USA Ryder Cup team. I nearly had a chance to see him play at Wentworth in 1956 when he was playing in the Canada Cup (now the World Cup), which he and his partner Sam Snead won.

I asked two of my professional colleagues who were there just how impressed they were with Hogan; not so much with his play, although they agreed it was very professional, but more with his ability to concentrate and his superhuman patience.

'For example', they told me, 'play was painfully slow, with as much as twenty minutes' wait on some tees. On one tee, with such a gap in play, and while his three playing companions were fidgeting around and chatting to the gallery, Hogan stood in front of the tee quite motionless for the whole time, like some Red Indian outside his wigwam, his eyes unwaveringly rivetted on the spot on the fairway where he eventually hit his drive.'

NICKLAUS OPTION

The familiar swing of Jack Nicklaus illustrates perfectly all the common factors that support and embellish the correct basic mechanics.
Opposite, top left: The assembly involves a solid base, an upright posture and a firm grip which also allows those joints used in the swing to function properly.
Top centre: The backswing path is directly away from target, while his base is held securely to permit him to coil round his spine and so begin the collection of optimum potential energy.
Top right: The top of the backswing shows the optimum coil within his

tolerance. He has suffered no loss of centre – nor any undue strain, for he can't afford to risk damaging muscles or joints. His hands and wrists are 'adducted' to centre (see page 64).

Bottom left: *The retention of the wrist angle he collected in the backswing is conserving the speed in the clubhead on the forward swing. The later he releases the faster it will be released, though it mustn't be a fraction too late. The path of the forward swing is nearer to him than was the backswing, which counteracts the changing position of the body.*

Bottom centre and right: *Much of the forward swing is 'spontaneous' but the centering is controlled to permit the left side to wind spirally after contact. He then comes up gradually after contact to allow the acceleration of the swing unit, an essential factor for the balance which he so strikingly displays. In other words, he has successfully contained the torque which his tremendous speed of swing generates.*

Before Hogan began to win tournaments he had many years of hard practice and financial worry.

As a pupil try to develop Hogan's patience. You won't get near his ability to practise eight to ten hours a day, but cultivate an enjoyment for practice and you will then get more benefit from it. Being observant and asking questions of your teacher to clarify your understanding of his advice will upgrade you as a learner and a player, too. Expect it to take a certain amount of time – and enjoy the challenge.

Time and practice

My 'Forward Drive' method is not a magic formula for a quick and easy way to play golf. On the contrary, it tends to take time and patience before the ingredients mix into a smooth and effective machine. But there's one thing I can say for sure: when those ingredients are properly blended they will produce golf shots as good as you can reasonably hope for within your physical and mental tolerances.

It will add length to your shots because it tracks the clubhead for a moment longer along the target line and holds it fleetingly longer into the back of the ball than the wristy method – if it's allowed to.

It will add nothing to your length if you're striving with might and main to hit the ball further. I've said it often: the long hitters just hit the ball a long way, while the short hitters are continually trying to.

There are quick ways of learning – I have no doubt about that. To quote Irv, 'There's a high rate of "forgetting".' I always suspect too, that the faster the student's rise, the faster the fall will be! I think it's possible to *explain* how to play in a matter of minutes. Certainly some people think they can learn to play golf in not much more than that time. It all depends on what you mean by *playing* golf.

You are not really 'playing' until the swing is a habit which gives you an acceptably high percentage of good shots. And achieving this enjoyable objective demands a certain amount of time and practice.

I once told a millionaire customer of mine that he would have to work at his golf before he would be able to enjoy it. 'I didn't come here to work, I came here for pleasure', he replied. I asked him how he made his money. 'By working', he answered. 'Do you enjoy your money?' I enquired. 'Yes', he said mirthfullly, 'and I'll hit you with this bloody club . . !' I stepped back, but he had taken my point.

CHAPTER TWO

THE ORIGINS
OF FORWARD DRIVE

I reckon I've spent more than half my adult life picking other peoples' brains, and the other half digesting and making use of the information I have gleaned. So I'd like to take this opportunity of making a general acknowledgement to everyone who helped me to formulate my teaching methods before I met Irvin Schloss. All were professionals with the exception of John Pennock, whose observations brought to my attention that common superstar factor of *flow*, or 'the swing without the conscious hit', and the late Doug Graham, lecturer in psychology at Durham University, who helped me understand the limits of psychology in golf.

When I gave my first lesson I was 16 years of age, and my pupil was a young man in his mid-twenties. I'd not even started 'brain-picking' then. I had no such information at my fingertips, and no mechanical knowledge of the golf swing, when my father hustled me out to the practice area by the side of the first fairway at the Saltburn-by-the-Sea Golf Club in north-east Yorkshire. He was the professional there, and I was his self-appointed and extremely enthusiastic assistant.

Strangely enough I can't recall having any qualms about my ability to put that first fellow right, even though he was a four-handicap player! I can't even remember what he was doing wrong – but I do remember successfully correcting his swing. It didn't seem too awesome a task for me. Big-headed, you may think. But I simply used the aesthetic picture I had of a golf swing, and compared it with that of my 'pupil'. When and where the latter didn't coincide with the former I took the difference or differences and changed them into that mental picture.

It worked for the most part, so I didn't have too many failures on my conscience, but my conscience was not always so crystal clear in the years that followed.

My father had an excellent reputation as a teacher. He was a very strong man, and even with hickory-shafted clubs he could hit the ball prodigious distances. He was also a clubmaker with a penchant for experimentation, particularly with insets for woods, especially drivers.

I tried hard to pick my father's brains, but to no avail. With him it was 'do as I say and ask no questions'. This suited a lot of people, but I was unable 'not to reason why'. Having said that, I still learned a lot from him about teaching, particularly about the plane of the golf swing, the Vardon grip and a wide backswing. I was prone to narrow down my own backswing. I didn't try to do anything special at the top of the backswing, nor can I remember teaching more than keeping the grip firm there.

'Early release'

My mechanics were simply based on a swing rather than a hit, and even in those days I liked to think that the hands beat the clubhead to the ball before contact. In other words, I was teaching what might be described as a 'late release'. I don't honestly think that I was conscious of using this term, otherwise I might have latched on to 'early release'. I certainly remember letting the clubhead overtake the hands at the right time. I could hit longer shots this way if I wanted to.

You needn't be perfect to be a great golfer. Fred Couples defies convention with his cupped left wrist and 'flying' right elbow, and it follows that he must make huge compensations on his forward swing rather than simply respond to his unique backswing. This is fine if the player knows exactly what those movements should be, and Couples obviously does, for he gets terrific right-hand reaction into the ball to produce drives of prodigious length. At the top of the backswing his feet are still firmly on the ground, and apart from the unusual position of his arms and hands he has remained in perfect equilibrium, set to change direction without loss of centre, balance or speed.

I was blissfully ignorant that most of my local colleagues were teaching an 'open face' at the top with cupped wrists, probably the effects of a much earlier 'wrist angle collection' than I taught. That is, the clubface was pointed not to the sky but to the horizon in front of the player, with the back of the left hand flexed towards the wristwatch face. The picture of Fred

Couples on page 18 graphically illustrates this. By the time the swing had been returned to hip high, the clubhead had to be virtually 'thrown at the ball' in order to return it to a square-faced contact. As I said, I'd not previously recognized a specific position at the top of the backswing.

I was then professional to the Whitley Bay Golf Club in Northumberland and John Long, a former pro who was doing a part-time job assisting me in the shop, brought this 'other' method to my notice. It was around then that I felt I might have been wrong. But how on earth could I put this over to my pupils?

I have never taught anything to my pupils without first trying it myself. This has nothing to do with being subjective. I still make these tests with every new idea I may come up with or that I hear about, if it has merit. What's more, if there's an appreciable difference from my normal system, I give it a long trial of at least six months, possibly a year. So I didn't plunge into change impulsively.

When I played with my colleagues in the local events, using the 'new' concept, I got some remarkable observations from them, but I was surprised these professionals couldn't spot this deliberately early release, maybe because it was 'natural' for them to use it. And this was the point: a lot of professionals were in fact playing this way with modest success. They may not have been winning international or national events but there were plenty of very good golfers using this 'clubhead throwing' way of playing. It did in fact require great skill. It's by no means a wrong way of playing, albeit somewhat 'cavalier'.

Getting 'hooked' on a new concept

In due course I tried it out on a few new students. It worked particularly well with the ladies, but as in everything else most golfers are asked to do, they usually over-emphasized. All too soon they were throwing the clubhead from the top of the swing or even before that, if it is possible, digging holes as much as a foot behind the ball. The Americans call this 'drop kicking' – and this was 'drop kicking' with a vengeance.

I don't think I was beginning to hit as early as these students of mine; but the time came when this long draw with the low flying rightward take-off, culminating in a pleasant leftward swerve to target, deteriorated into a simple hook of almighty proportions. My hand action was not skilful enough for the perfect timing this whiplash style demanded.

The question now arose of how to cure the hook. It was simple enough, really: lead longer with the hands, lag the clubhead if you like. But wait a moment, wasn't this where I came in – late release? Wasn't that how I started before that fellow disturbed my innocent ignorance?

The late Syd Scott, then the pro at nearby Hartlepool, suggested to me that the backswing path for the early release method, which is usually taken deliberately inside from the 'take-off', could trigger off a tendency for the forward swing to go too abruptly inside after contact. Hence the hook. He advocated taking a straight line back past the right foot!

This coincided with the discussion I had with former French and Irish Open champion Bert Gadd about his own backswing start (which I have detailed a little later in this chapter), and helped to confirm my original principles. And it led to my abandonment of the early release system.

It was when Tommy Aaron was a young member of the United States Walker Cup team at Muirfield in 1959 that Bill Cox pointed out the 'neutral' position of the clubface at the top of his backswing. The more 'open' face associated with the wristier actions needs skilful compensation to bring it back squarely to the ball. To me the American's style was evidence of another method, one which most British pros had seen little or nothing of before. This was the so-called '1.68 ball swing', since the small ball was still mainly in use in Britain during the 1950s.

A long chat I had while watching the 1959 Walker Cup at Muirfield with W. J. (Bill) Cox, then one of Britain's top teachers, drew my attention to the neutral faced position of the clubface at the top of Tommy Aaron's backswing. By neutral I mean the face of the club and the back of the left hand are at 45° to the sky. A wristy action tends to 'open' the face of the club a lot, pointing it more down to the ground, and this also 'cups' the left wrist. Being less open, the former is more economical, but the latter contains extra movements, and so needs applied and skilful compensations to bring the clubface back squarely to the ball.

I now used the new backswing and the neutral clubface position at the top of it, and I found that these worked really well for my students, too.

I was always fascinated by Bert Gadd's 'take-away', for he seemed, like Lee Trevino, to take a path outside the target line when he started back. But he claimed it was along the target line, and my own movie sequence of him proved him right. The coil of the body obviously takes the path inside and away from the target line.

In effect of course, Trevino takes a direct from target path back, but his open stance (left foot drawn back from right) makes it appear to be 'outside' the target line, as Bert Gadd's did.

When I eventually discovered through Irv Schloss that a 'directly' back line was a common factor of those international superstars who are legends in their lifetime – Hogan, Snead, Palmer, Player and Nicklaus – I felt my early choice of a 'straight back', in feel at least, was clearly vindicated. But I was later to be wrapped over the knuckles by Irv for using the expression 'straight back'. He mentioned that I should (and I think he was right) use 'directly back'. From now on I would do so.

'Throwing tradition to the wind'

I was an avid reader of the *Golf Monthly* magazine especially of the articles of Irv Schloss which, I'm pleased to say, appeared regularly at that time in those venerable pages. In the December 1967 issue he enumerated five examples of what he called 'British' swing weaknesses. They were: 1 – unstable centering; 2 – wristiness-flicking; 3 – over application of energy related to the task; 4 – a too-early release on the downswing; 5 – a 'hanging left arm' on and beyond contact. Much to my delight, numbers 2 and 4 underlined what I was already teaching, and what I had already discarded. I found myself unequivocably agreeing with the other three examples of swing weaknesses.

If you think of the corrections to those weaknesses, only three are needed to resolve the five: 1 – centering is maintained by holding your right leg and foot in towards the left on the backswing and keeping the left side of your face to the right side of the ball until after contact on the forward swing; 2 – early release or 'wristiness' is reduced by letting your hands lead the clubhead through contact – left hand ahead of the right (or 'abduction'); 3 – the left arm is kept moving to target continuously to stop it from hanging limply through contact. The jigsaw was very gradually falling into place.

Interestingly, and prophetically, Schloss goes on to say that Tony Jacklin was one of the few British players displaying modern techniques. Less than two years later Jacklin won the Open and less than a year after that the US Open.

British star Mark James has an unorthodox backswing, but by 'leading with his hands' on the forward swing he's simply allowing the laws of circular motion to operate without human interference. The result is one of the best contacts in the game.

Schloss had taken films of some of our Ryder Cup stars' 'swings' and he sent them to the players concerned. He later met one of them on a visit to Britain, but he was surprised and disappointed to learn that he had never bothered to look at it.

'Your best teachers', said Irv Schloss, 'can learn more about the proven modern golf swing through high-speed cinematography, seminars, clinics, and schools like ours in the United States, where golf instruction is more advanced today than it was "yesterday", and it will be more advanced "tomorrow".

'This information could be made readily available to our professional brethren in Britain. The time has come for tradition to be thrown to the four winds. What was good enough for your forefathers should *not* be good enough for you.' He continued to say that he planned to return to Britain the following September. He would bring his films along and meet with any group of British professionals.

Completing the jigsaw: the swing on film

In many respects that meeting changed my life for the better. Strangely enough, though Schloss had completely confirmed the principles of my teaching, in a perverse way I almost wished he had not, for I think I was looking for something different to give me a fresh start. I certainly admired and envied his energy, enthusiasm, knowledge and his completely mechanical and logical approach.

But that was it of course: he *had* given me something new. I could emulate his drive and use his mechanics to amplify my aesthetics.

It was now not only how a swing looked, but also whether it kept within the limits of the laws of physics. He had put all those remaining pieces into their places. The jigsaw was complete. Well, almost. I certainly needed to become an expert at both cine and still photography. I've made good progress but, as with my teaching, I'm forever eager to learn more.

In anticipation of any queries about video, I can only say that video does not yet provide the precision, X-ray analysis of a golf swing that 16mm or even 8mm cine photography does, when they are properly used.

I wasn't completely satisfied that my ideas on the psychology of golf could stand the test, however. My views needed clarifying and my trip to the United States four years later practically settled the issue for me. After hearing the fascinating Hubie Smith lecture (reproduced in chapter 13) I was convinced that his professional approach of common sense and self-discipline just about says it all.

Tightening the technique

It's well worth looking at this 'technique tightening' which emerged from that long, film-backed lecture by Irv Schloss, in London nearly twenty years ago. It left me with a teaching plan which in my view all golf teachers should adopt. In fact, with the American schools and now the British PGA schools advocating a similar formula, I'm sure most teachers already do this.

Briefly the headings are as follows:

Lesson procedure

1. Conversation (with student, to 'weigh him up').
2. Examination (watching student play shots to assess his strengths and weaknesses).
3. Explanation (of student's faults or faults and what he has to do for correction, *modifying* them and *minimizing* the change).
4. Demonstration (by teacher, explaining exactly what student has to do).
5. Imitation (by student).
6. Correction (by teacher).
7. Repetition (so the student leaves clearly understanding his task).

The swing formula

1. Aim; grip; stance; posture.
2. Centering.
3. Expansion.
4. Plane.
5. Movement sequence.
6. Winding; torque; return response.
7. Finish (high, no breakdown).

Combined with the understanding of plane I had a sound framework from which to teach, out of which I need not stray, but which still left me with enough scope for any new ideas. Playing methodically within a system is the only way to minimize 'form fluctuation', on which I shall go into detail later.

The term 'forward drive' came out of a late night session on the swing with Percy Huggins, then editor of *Golf Monthly* magazine. I hope that in the chapters that follow it will provide you with a key to improving your game.

Before describing my own method, I must say that I'm not taking issue with those of other teachers, be they flickers, rollers, free-wheelers, stylists (everyone different), 'squares', subjectivists or 'do-your-own-thing' merchants. I've gone through the whole spectrum and I've yet to be convinced that any of these can give my students or myself the slightest advantage. As I have said before, however, the moment I realize that something better has arisen and been proved beyond doubt, then I will unashamedly forsake my convictions of a lifetime.

How 'natural' is the golf swing?

When you hear players talking about the natural way to play you may have no doubt about what they mean. It's likely you will see someone who, to all intents and purposes, plays golf well without conscious method or thought, without practice and care.

But I wonder if these players who profess to be natural really are? Do they know what 'natural' means?

Have you ever noticed how a young boy gets holds of a golf club for the first time in his life and tries to hit the golf ball? Look at the picture on page 25. The separated grip, with the left hand *below* the right, and the vertical chopping movement as though the child is using a pickaxe, is as natural as you can get.

Almost every infant will adopt this caveman attitude. And if it is any consolation, it is possible, even likely, that Jack Nicklaus and Tom Watson began their golfing careers by wielding a club in just this way. What follows then, must necessarily be an almost complete change of 'natural tendencies'.

Youngsters taking up the game see golfers of all levels playing, if not on courses then certainly on television. This will lead to a good deal of conscious and subconscious imitation which triggers off the mechanical process of learning the swing and thus effectively manages to 'by pass' nature.

Whether you're three or 19, the swing is a serious business, but which one of these is the more 'natural' action? If it's any consolation to us lesser mortals, it's almost certain that Ballesteros and Norman began their careers by using the 'cackhanded' grip employed here by my step-grandson Stephen, with the left hand below the right. I think the picture illustrates the point that the swing is to a large extent a manufactured action, and Ulf Nilsson, a former pupil of mine and now one of Sweden's rising tide of hopeful young professionals, had to learn the hard way, as we all do. Both lads share a well extended left arm which collects a good deal of potential energy – and I like Stephen's slightly raised left heel, often a characteristic of somewhat more rotund adults.

CHAPTER THREE

FORWARD DRIVE: POWER GOLF FOR ALL

Taking aim

It's natural, of course, to take aim before you're going to hit, drive or fire anything at a target, but there's also a very natural temptation in golf to be casual about it. Professionals tend to be far more fastidious in this respect than amateurs, who can often take it rather for granted or hurry it, particularly on a busy course. On the practice areas a lot of pros put a club

or clubs on the ground pointing to the target, or in matches they have the caddie constantly check their lining up of the shot.

It is, however, the crucial first step in any shot, and aiming routine should be practised until it becomes a habit you never lose. You take your target line from behind the ball rather than from the swing position and you aim with your clubface rather than with your shoulders. The 'cross and arrow' is useful for fixing your aim and adjusting your stance.

Getting the correct grip

Having taken aim, you should then carefully fix the grip. You'll see more bad grips in amateur golf than in the professional game, because in my view the amateur will put comfort first whereas the professional use mechanics as the basis for gripping.

This practice ground device called the 'cross and arrow', demonstrated here by my assistant Brian Davies, can be bought at many pro shops. The two small and easily portable metal devices are excellent for fixing your aim mathematically and adjusting your stance relative to it. Constantly aiming correctly soon becomes a welcome habit, but it should never be taken for granted, no matter what the circumstances.

Opposite: *Professionals tend to be far more careful about taking aim than amateurs, and this shot of 1986 USPGA champion Bob Tway making sure of his target line during a practice session should prove instructive for many a hurried club golfer. I can't emphasize too much the importance of correct aim; if your aim is wrong you must swing badly in a futile attempt at correction.*

I'm going to break my vow of objectivity here and say that when I take my grip, it still does not feel comfortable; but *it feels right*. If I let it resolve into a more relaxed position it certainly feels comfortable – but I know it's not right.

I was once taking a group of beginners at an evening class in the north-east of England for 12 two-hourly lessons before Christmas and another 12

Jack Nicklaus uses the interlocking grip, or at least a hybrid of the original, which had the thumbs outside. In conventional style, his left thumb is tucked into his right hand. The right forefinger and thumb 'trigger' and the two to three knuckles which he has showing the back of his left hand are both common factors of the top professionals' grip.

after Christmas, and one lady had considerable difficulty grappling with her grip. On the last evening, just before the end of the lesson, she came along for a final grip check. Her fingers were almost inextricably entangled round the shaft. It took me quite some time to unravel them so that I could once more, perhaps for the hundredth time, place them correctly for her.

'Mr Cooke,' she pleaded, 'I know this is the right way, but it's too uncomfortable.'

I emphasized the importance of the finger grip pressure, especially on the last three left-hand fingers; but I must add that I've yet to see a great player who doesn't grip firmly and lightly *but* not tightly or loosely, with the triggered right forefinger and thumb. I have a view about the so-called 'long left thumb': if the left thumb is too long it will force the shaft into the palms and prise open the right thumb and forefinger trigger. Having just stressed the importance of retaining a relatively firm right-hand trigger, need I say more? Except, perhaps, that I prefer the 'retracted' thumbs.

I'm not in favour of teaching a weak grip, with the left hand gripping under the shaft to the left and the right hand very much on top. This is recommended by some players and coaches, who feel that if a youngster can make his swing draw the ball softly, despite having a 'fader's' grip, he will become a better golfer. In fact most of the superstars started their golf with a draw grip, the left hand wrapped round a little more to the right, and became highly skilful at producing the 'soft draw'. The ball starts just right of target and finally swerves gently leftward into target.

When they became bored with this they cultivated the very opposite flight, starting slightly left and fading right into target. To achieve this they 'weakened' the left-hand grip. It's quite possible to produce this left-to-right shot by a slight turn of the clubface at assembly. A draw *could* be produced by an opposite twist, but I prefer to teach my pupils to draw the ball with a stronger left hand, more to the right, which activates a rotation or winding of the arms and hands at the right time and in the right direction.

Weight and pressure: getting down to the job

In the past I've advocated 'getting down to the ball' with the knees. After a good deal more experiment and experience I'm now completely convinced that you should start off with your legs straight and get down to the ball from the waist, or with a spinal angle, as much as the club you're using demands, before finally flexing the knees a *little* towards the ball and a *little* from the insides of the knees towards each other.

Having said that, I must warn you that getting down from the waist must not involve getting down or slumping from the shoulders with your chin tucked into your chest. Your feet should grip the ground mainly from the insides of the soles of the shoes so that the pressure and weight is all along the insides of your feet from the heels to the toes; thus the ground grips you and you grip the ground.

Some teachers tend to favour the pressure and weight being towards the toes, while others favour it being towards the heels. It has been necessary on occasion for me to advise a student to increase the pressure and weight on the toes when perhaps for some reason there is too much on the heels, and vice versa for another student. As a broad generalization, however, the distribution of pressure and weight between each foot and leg should be about even. Some teachers advise 60 per cent right and 40 per cent left; some even advise 75 per cent right and 25 per cent left, reversing this on the short shots. But my '50–50' recommendation is applicable for both the full shots and the short ones. The swing responses to this are invariably more uniform and correct.

In my view if there is a preponderance of pressure and weight on the right foot at assembly then it will be more difficult, though not impossible, to shed all this to the left foot on the forward swing. If there is a

The author demonstrates the correct way to set the club down to the ball.
The pros place the club behind the ball and bend the spine down from the
waist to accommodate the lie of the club (left), placing its sole on the ground
with a slightly raised toe. The less experienced amateur tends to get the club
down to the ball by sinking his knees (right), leading to a very cramped
assembly lacking in space.

preponderance of pressure and weight on the left foot at assembly, the response on the forward swing would be to tend to shed this to the right foot.

The backswing response to too much weight and pressure on either foot would be likely to cause tilting or swaying, or both. An even distribution of pressure and weight, however, would facilitate a centered and balanced coil with practically no change of the even assembly spread all the way back.

The position of the head

The head position at assembly has provoked a few theories and arguments. It's been said that: 1 – it is better to set the chin tilted a little towards the left; 2 – to look straight at the ball; 3 – to tilt the chin a little to the right; 4 – to start by looking straight at the ball and then tilt the chin a little to the right just before or just on starting the swing.

The advocates of the first theory say that this makes it easier to turn the shoulders; the advocates of the second say that this makes centering easier; the advocates of the third say that this makes the shoulder turn easier, as do those who plump for the fourth.

I'm of the 'second' school, but I'm sympathetic to the adherents of the last. I've yet to fathom why, if the chin has a leftward tilt, this could facilitate a rightward turn of the shoulders. It seems to me that long before the left shoulder turns its required 90° it will collide with the chin!

Keep the left side of your face, your left cheek, just to the right of the golf ball, until the ball has gone; that's as simple and all-embracing a formula for 'centering and uncoiling' that could possibly be devised.

The stance

Your hands should be near to your left thigh as opposed to being too far away from it. Your upper arms, grooved to your upper torso, should leave your forearms clear of your lower body. Your elbows squeezed gently towards each other will compact the swing triangle of your arms and shoulders, with your left arm and shaft almost in a straight line, and the necessarily sunken wrists will accommodate the contact area effect of centrifugal force.

It's perhaps significant that the supporters of the 'spread arms' system at assembly straighten them almost immediately they move into the dynamic part of the swing. You have to weigh the advantages of this against the disadvantages before falling into the rather soft embrace of the spread-armed assembly.

If you forget to draw in your elbows, you will be left with a spreadeagled swing – with its attendant 'eyrie of errors'. On the other hand, moving from a soft-armed start to a firm, compacted swing might add to your collection of potential energy.

Your wrists should be slightly sunk (to accommodate the effects of centrifugal force). Your legs should be wide enough to be within the bounds of comfort, with your knees flexed in from the insides towards each other. The base from your knees to your feet should grip the ground all along the insides of the shoes. There are two schools of thought here. One says that the feet should be solidly planted; the other says they should be gripping the ground but alert and springy, ready for the 'off'. I favour the latter condition, but there is nothing wrong in a flat-footed assembly and a flat-footed backswing. Your chin should be up and centered or tilted only a little towards the right shoulder, so the forehead will tilt equally towards the left shoulder.

The assemblies of Sam Snead, Bruce Crampton, Gary Player and Tommy Aaron demonstrate the following common factors. A stance wider than the shoulders that provides a firm base on which to swing in good balance. The club face looks up to the ball, not down as with so many handicap players. The left arm is predominant and in a continuous line with the shaft of the club. I call this the 'swing radius'. The hands are not ahead of the ball. They will be at contact, thus making a physical 'gain'. The arms are neither loose nor spread. They come quite firmly down from the shoulders. The posture is up, commanding and solid, not down or loose.

As a generalization a narrow stance favours the 'wristy' method, while a wide stance favours the 'non-wristy' method.

'Non-wristy' doesn't mean there's no wrist movement involved, of course. On the backswing there's a wrist response and on the forward swing there's wrist retention and 'timed release'. There's also a wrist response to the effect of centrifugal force.

A wide stance should be comfortably wide and form a secure base to support the actions involved in a golf swing. A stance that is narrower than the shoulders will necessarily be 'top heavy' and less likely to be well-balanced.

Ball position

My own view of the ball position in relation to the feet coincides with the Irv Schloss method. For the shorter clubs, up to a six-iron, the ball is placed in the middle of the feet, and from the five-iron to the two-iron it should be positioned progressively towards the left heel. All the woods should be opposite the left heel. The middle is a very safe position.

Another and for some a quite attractive school of thought advocates positioning the ball opposite the left heel for *all* shots, and then widening the right foot as the clubs get 'longer'.

It's safe to say that you'll see very few pro stars who are not properly assembled in every respect, allowing for such rare idiosyncracies as the low hands of Hubert Green and the outside-the-ball clubhead of Fuzzy Zoeller. And yet, even as they conform to orthodoxy, each is easily recognizable as they complete the preparation – and even more so as the swing becomes dynamic.

Assembly: a summary

Golf is very different from the 'moving ball games' such as baseball, cricket and tennis, where you react to the ball coming towards you. The golfer has complete control over the state of the ball when he hits it, and in this fundamental sense he has no excuse; he cannot blame the pitcher, the bowler or a great serve from his opponent across the net. It is, perhaps, one of the basic reasons for its being such an intriguing challenge. You *can* aim for perfection.

You have plenty of time in golf to assemble yourself, and every position is important. The dynamic part of the swing tends to respond to the static, so make the static a 'conscious constant'. When you know what each position is for, how the swing responds to it and why, you will have learned a big lesson in golf.

So, let me summarize the assembly:
1. Aim, grip and stance, in that order.
2. Aim with the face of the club.
3. Your toes and shoulders should be parallel to the target line.
4. Your hips should be twisted slightly left (to tighten the coil on the backswing and to facilitate the uncoiling on the forward swing).
5. Let your shoulders hang 'naturally' as opposed to being hunched.
6. Your upper arms should be touching your body but your lower arms should be clear of you.
7. Your left arm should be extended downwards and your right elbow flexed comfortably in towards your left elbow.

CHAPTER FOUR

PICKING UP THE RHYTHM

There are many way of 'moving away', but only a few variations on the same theme are actually acceptable.

In this day and age you could be forgiven for assuming that the 'waggle', the preliminary gesture which took a more prominent part in the older-fashioned swings, mainly to promote 'feel', was defunct. But if you watch a professional tournament you'll be hard pressed to find any players, including the big names, who don't make a distinct movement to initiate the swing.

I can remember teaching my beginners to 'waggle' in the shape of a capital P. 'Up the stem, clockwise round the loop, and down the stem again.' This of course describes a shape which you would draw in the space around the ball with the clubhead, with your arms via your hands.

Obviously there are an infinite variety of waggles, and some can be a mite destructive if the main movement is away from the normal flow of the ensuing swing.

The simplest form is to take the club from its assembly position behind the ball along the target line, directly back from target for a foot or so, maybe less, and back to the ball again.

Usually the completion of the waggle is determined by a 'forward press', that is, to target. This is either a slight flexing of the hands or arms in the direction of the target, or the hips, knees and hands. Again, this so-called 'forward press' is a self-evident phenomenon of the pros and superstars. Its function is to inaugurate rhythm into the swing. The crucial point is that it makes a 'live' start to the swing instead of a 'dead' one.

Famous 'waggles'

Waggles and forward presses often characterize famous players. Gary Player has a distinctive right knee genuflexion to the left, to target; Arnold Palmer pushes a less obtrusive right side reminder to target; Jack Nicklaus has a short staccato-like waggle confined mainly to his hands, and his pre-swing intentions seem to be more centered on determining his intermediate target about two feet from the ball, his eyes rivetting themselves a number of times from the ball to this target. None of the great players will now be too conscious of these preliminaries, but it's unlikely that these habitual actions will ever be omitted.

Gary Player's characteristic 'knee kick-start' triggers his move from the static into the dynamic, setting the rhythm for the rest of his swing. His hands move back with the club. There is no wristy pick up.

I recommend some sort of flourish as a prelude to the swing because it can prime the swing rhythm. It should be short, simple and partially trace the intended path of the swing to come. It's important to remember that once the waggle has been completed and you have brought the clubhead back to rest behind the ball, you should not delay for more than a count of three before moving into action.

The forward press which sparks the dynamism should be slight rather than overdone. You can disrupt the whole of the carefully prepared assembly by making a 'lunge' of a forward press.

Practising a forward press, like practising a waggle, means having to think about it, of course. But after enough practice, it should become habit and it will happen automatically. The only time it will vary – and you will have to be on your guard against this – is under various pressures, in a competition or when somebody is watching. The shape of your waggle and your forward press will only be slightly affected, but your rhythm could become hurried and snatchy in the first case and, conversely, over-deliberate under the eagle eye of an onlooker you wished were miles away.

It's not sensible for an experienced player to be too concerned about these 'trigger' movements. If as an experienced player you've never cultivated them, there could be little value in adding them to a well-established and successful swing. If you do have them already, it is unlikely, but possible, that they may need directional or shape or pace correction such as 'from hurried to leisurely'.

Into the dynamics of the swing

Starting back should come directly from the arms through the medium of the hands. There should be no conscious wrist action; I'd go so far as to say there should be 'consciously no wrist action' in this early part of the swing.

Coupled with this there should be no premature flexion of the right elbow. It should not be hugged or pulled into the right side but kept as extended as it was at the assembly, until it's acted on by the effects of continuity, clubweight and inertia when, with the wrists, it's forced to bend. This not only tracks the clubhead on the widest possible arc, but also helps to supply the backswing with its optimum amount of potential energy.

It should seem very much like taking the whole of the arms, hands and golf club assembly position directly back from the target without changing it at all, while still holding the base with your feet. The clubface should look at the ball before it naturally begins to 'fan' gradually away from it.

The 'natural' part of the club fanning to the right away from the ball owes much of its existence to the forearm bones (the radius and ulna). These bones rotate clockwise as the arms extend back. The rest of the rotation is influenced by the coil of the body. In effect the clubface, although originally held onto the ball, progressively turns away from it. You can deliberately 'hood' the face to modify this natural rotation, especially to counteract excessive fanning.

Miller Barber, a top American star, is one of the few examples of habitual and very exaggerated clubface 'hooding' in the early stages of the golf swing, and it works well for him. Ben Hogan had a period when he capitalized on cupping his left wrist, thus opening his clubface during the course of the backswing. Tom Kite appears to 'add flames to the fire' by fanning more than naturally. And no-one can say he hasn't made a good job of it.

'Flail' action

The delayed wrists and right elbow angling inaugurate the flail action which most of the professional players use. This is the same as that used in the olden days to thresh corn with a flail. This needed an upward swing of the flail with the hands pulling the flail up and a downward swing with the hands leading the flail down. In the golf swing the movement is from side to side. You can imagine how unsuccessful it would have been to hinge with a flail – that is, the flail 'leading' the hands.

There's a school of thought which advocates initiating the swing from the shoulders by coiling them and letting the arms and wrists react. Another advises a preset wrist-angle collection which does at the beginning what the 'flail' does at the top.

PUTTING OFF THE STYLE

When it comes to learning about a method of playing golf, you have to settle for one school of thought. You'll have a patchwork mess if you meddle with them all. I once had an amateur partner in a national foursome event who stood on the 21st tee (our match had gone two holes over the 18 without decision) and said to me, 'I'm not sure whether to use the Vardon, Nelson or Hogan swing here.' I unwittingly said, 'Just use your own,' and he sliced the ball into thick rough. Fortunately, our opponents were even more indecisive and they went into the woods, and we were lucky to survive.

Working to a fixed pattern, one that has proved itself in general and in particular to the player, is a prerequisite for consistent results. At the same time it's important to recognize that no matter how sound a method may be, it will always be subject to the inevitable weaknesses in the human make-up.

Allowing for the vagaries of human nature, it's obviously better to adopt a proven method of playing than one that could be suspect. Not only would you have the unpredictability of human nature to cope with, but also the unsureness of the method if indeed, like my partner in the foursomes, you were trying something else.

Moreover, he was technically wrong in his imitation of any one player. He was trying to imitate *style*. You just can't do this; a player's style is his own. Ben Hogan will always look like Ben Hogan, Byron Nelson will always look like Byron Nelson, and Jack Nicklaus will always be distinguishable as Jack Nicklaus. I cannot remember my partner's choice on that occasion, but whoever it was, he looked, as ever, just like himself.

You can take the *common factors* of a number of star players. When combined, these can form a cohesive method of movement. And depending how well you coordinate them, these factors would work, relatively speaking, as well for you.

The 'shoulders school' has its merits but I'm not too happy about the possibilities of turning the shoulders against the hips and thus risking damage to the spine, or twisting the whole trunk off centre, either to the right or left, upwards or downwards.

The preset wrist position, cocking the wrists to initiate the backswing, can be useful if a student has difficulty in collecting any wrist and right elbow angle at all on the backswing, but I don't advocate deliberately 'creating' angles at any source.

An early collection of the wrist cock also automatically narrows down the size of the arc of the swing and prevents the optimum collection of potential energy in the backswing.

It's a fault to preset the left knee to start the backswing. From then on, it is a laborious affair which has more to do with lifting a long axe than swinging a golf club. The left knee flex and the elevation of the left heel should be a response, and a delayed one at that.

Transferring your weight

If the weight and pressure is evenly spread between the right and the left side in the assembly and the backswing coil is made on a centered vertical axis, it should follow that there would be little change of that weight and pressure at the top of the backswing, provided that the centre of the swing has been properly maintained.

The advocates of weight transference on the backswing are, in my opinion, putting their students in danger of swaying. But I must concede that there is a risk in every movement, even good ones. The over-diligent player trying *not* to transfer weight on the backswing might slip into the fault of transferring all the weight on to the left foot, culminating in a steep 'list to port' at the top of the backswing.

It is worth recapping on these first few feet of real activity. The hands should initiate the swing as a unit, taking the arms directly back from target *against* the knees! 'Against the knees' means that the legs from the knees down to the feet are held in, as you would hold the handle of a catapult as you are stretching the elastic. The wrist angle collection should be delayed. This not only begins the vital build up of potential energy but also starts the coil of the body from above the knees up to the shoulders.

CHAPTER FIVE

THE BACKSWING

With the continued extension of the arms 'against the knees' by halfway on the backswing, your body will be coiling from above the knees, both at the hips and shoulders. The hip coil should be 'direct', with no lateral movement but limited by the held base.

With most players the angling of the wrist will spontaneously begin at about 9 o'clock and be closely followed by the downward flexion of the right elbow. The pivotal point for the wrist angle collection is at the base of the thumbs. The more compact the grip, the nearer the pivotal points will be to each other and the more evenly they will flex. The shoulders, less affected by the lower body hold, will coil further than the hips by the time the backswing is completed.

The right leg should, to all intents and purposes, have remained as it began: a support column for holding the swing into centre. The left knee should have flexed towards the ball. The pressure along the inside of the left shoe should have transferred more to the ball of the foot. The left heel should have risen from the ground no more than one inch – and it is completely acceptable to keep it on the ground. If it gets too high off the ground the whole of the body coil loses its spring as well as jeopardizing the swing centre.

The top players vary in this. Ray Floyd elevates his left heel quite a lot on the backswing, and it helps him to coil better. Arnold Palmer hardly moves it at all, while Seve Ballesteros brings it off the ground just a little.

At the top of the backswing the clubshaft should be parallel to the target line. It would be acceptable to have it 'laid off' a shade to the left, but it should never cross the target line and point to the right of the target.

The swing should have been 'in plane' from no later than 9 o'clock, and ideally all the way back.

The plane of the backswing

There are three planes or 'tilts' acceptable within the spheres of human tolerance: flat, medium and upright. These are dictated mainly by the length and lie of the golf club you are using, but also to a certain degree by physique.

A short club (wedge) will create more waist angle at assembly and so you produce a more upright plane of the circle in the space around you with

The golf swing is practically useless without a plane or tilt. There are no great differences between the planes of the professionals: some are a little more flat than others, some a little more upright, but the vast majority are 'middle of the road'. It's important to remember that the type of club alone can make a significant change to the plane. When a pro alters his plane deliberately, there will be only a shadow of a difference between the original and the new.

With a driver, Ben Hogan (left) is demonstrably flatter than Gunnar Mueller with his sand-iron (right), while Ulf Nilsson is not quite halfway between the two with his 8-iron (centre). He would be, however, with a 5-iron. Notice how the longer club widens the angle of the arms from the body (see the section on the conical pendulum in chapter 10), which again affects the plane.

your arms via your hands. The golf swing is really that movement you make with your arms and hands; everything else is merely in support of this swing.

A medium-length club will create less waist bend than a wedge and therefore a less upright plane. This must mean a medium plane for medium-length clubs.

The longest club (the driver) will create the least waist angle of all the clubs and so a flatter plane will ensue.

Height influences but does not necessarily set the plane. For example, a shorter player is likely to stand further away from the ball than a taller player and would therefore make a flatter plane than the taller one, who would normally stand nearer to the ball and so would automatically adopt a more upright plane.

This does not change in the least the effect of the variation of the club lengths on any type of physique.

Jack Nicklaus is a perfect example of the benefits of an upright plane. In my view it keeps the club travelling along the target line longer than a medium plane, just as the medium plane holds it along that line longer than the flat plane does. You take your pick; none of the 'tilts' is wrong. Hogan used a flat plane and Trevino and Player employ medium planes, but all were tolerably flexible.

The important thing is that having set the plane, to keep in it, not only on the backswing but also on the forward swing. The pictures on page 40 illustrate how to 'check' your plane.

Many players, including professionals, believe that the plane of the swing is related to the space around the player and not to the ground. They're right. Once you understand plane it is remarkably simple to apply it. It's amazing how fluid the swing becomes when it is 'consciously' (and so actually) in a constant plane.

When it is only occasionally in plane – by accident rather than design – this could solve the mystery of why you could not repeat the smoothness of the odd super shot which tantalizingly pops up now and again and brings you back to the course or practice ground for more.

I rate plane very highly in importance in the golf swing. It is essential if you are going to achieve your maximum enjoyment from the game.

The professionals will be concerned a lot about the swing plane. Rightly or wrongly, and not always rightly, some will try to adopt a flatter plane, others a more upright plane, possibly on the recommendation of a tour colleague. I recently heard of a famous player recommending a flatter plane to a lesser but still quite well-known younger player because the former was of the opinion that this would make the younger player more consistent. Many teachers, and I am among them, would say that an upright swing that stays within reasonable limits must produce more consistent results because it tracks the clubhead longer along the target line than a flatter plane.

A change of plane, by the way, must involve an assembly change. A flatter plane means standing farther away from the ball than for an upright swing, or altering the lie of the clubs.

The backswing: a summary
1. Stretch your arms with your hands, directly back from the target against your knees.
2. Hold your centre by keeping your right foot and knee held in to the top of the swing as they were at the start.
3. Swing into 'plane' by halfway back and maintain that plane.

4. Do not rush it: a controlled pace will help your left side to 'coil' round your spine more effectively.
5. Your shoulder will have coiled 90°, your hips 45°.
6. The body coil really starts from above the knees, the thighs activating the hips and then the shoulders. The spine must be twisted involuntarily to a certain extent.
7. The face of the club should gradually turn away from the ball later rather than earlier in the backswing, but it can be allowed to turn away or 'fan out' earlier.

There must be an equal and opposite 'closing' of the clubface on the forward swing in response to any opening of it on the backswing; and there must be an equal and opposite opening of the clubface on the forward swing in response to any closing or 'hooding' of it on the backswing.

Alternatives to the 'forward drive' backswing

Let me divert now, for there are other ways of swinging back than my 'forward drive' method. One I stumbled across recently went something like this: you take the club back and around your feet in a circle, the plane related to the ground. This is originated by turning the shoulders regardless of centre loss. It was prescribed as a cure for slicing. You then return the clubhead on exactly the same path as you took it back!

Two young students of mine were originally taught this way. Both had certainly cured their slice – but instead had developed huge hooks. It needed just a couple of corrections to readjust to my 'wheel system' before they began to hit straight shots.

A lot of senior golfers fall into the trap of deliberately shortening their backswing under the illusion that they will increase their swing control. Nothing could be further from the truth. A shortened backswing makes for a shortened coil and loss of potential energy, among a host of evils.

If you cannot lengthen it or coil more (against that base) leave well alone. The advancing years may or may not cause subconscious or real shortening because of physical limitations, but let your body make its own adjustments when it has to. Keep within your tolerances, but don't celebrate a birthday by limiting them.

At the top of the backswing

During the pause at the top of the backswing – and there has to be one if you're going to change direction – the following criteria should apply:
1. You should be perfectly in balance.
2. The upper part of your body should be coiled or 'wound' against the lower part. Your legs below the knees have been held as a platform or base for your arms to stretch against. Stretch as opposed to contract.

At the top of his backswing with a short iron Greg Norman is perfectly centred. While his coil is not so pronounced as it would be with a longer club, he has nevertheless collected enough potential energy to fuel the rest of the movement, using essentially an upright plane. He demonstrates a surprising degree of grace for such a powerfully built player. Yet in a sense grace and power go together; the more graceful, the more powerful. A large engine must generate more energy than a small one built on similar principles.

COTTON AND HOGAN: SYMBOLS OF US AND BRITISH METHODS
Henry Cotton had as wide a backswing as his contemporary Ben
Hogan. His plane was actually a little more upright, but strangely
enough, while Hogan had a flattish left wrist and hand line at the top
of the backswing, Cotton's was very slightly cupped. Hogan's
clubface was distinctly open, though you would have expected it to be
neutral or closed with the uncupped left wrist. Cotton's clubface was
neutral to closed, though with a cupped left wrist you would expect
the clubface to be open.

The contradiction here is explained in the grip: Cotton had a weak
left-hand grip, with barely one knuckle showing, while Hogan had a
strong left-hand grip with two or three knuckles showing. Cotton's
right hand was slightly more over to the left than Hogan's.

Both men closed the clubface onto the golf ball, but each very
differently. Cotton crossed his right arm over the left *against* the left
arm, with emphasis on the wrists; his legs played little part in this.
Hogan delayed this crossover longer than Cotton, mainly because his
legs played a much more active part in the forward swing, and his *left*
arm predominated with much less wrist involvement.

If the two were ever seen playing together, it would have seemed to
the knowledgeable onlooker that Hogan used his legs much more
obviously than Cotton. Cotton looked, and was, the 'wristier' player.

Paradoxically, both thought of themselves as 'open to closed'
players, but Cotton was more correct than Hogan in his self-analysis.
He did open the clubface on the backswing, and it was pointing
directly to the horizon in front of him. Hogan's clubface was pointing
$45°$ to the sky. Both retained their wrist angles on the forward swing
but, of necessity, Hogan held his longer than Cotton. In other words
Cotton had more open clubface to close than Hogan. Naturally the
former had to begin closing earlier, and the latter had to be later.

3. Your arms are extended only in feel, but in fact your right arm is flexed.
4. Your hands are still firmly in control of the club (which is parallel to the
   target line), by virtue of adducted wrist flex into centre.
5. Your right leg, tilted into centre, supports the trunk coil and has thus
   insured a hip turn instead of a hip slide or lateral shift.
6. Your left knee has semi-circled until the knee-cap is pointing to the ball.
   The heel can be on the ground or very slightly off it.
7. The muscular condition is firmly 'wound' under controlled tension. It's
   springy and alert, not relaxed, loose or sloppy.

Henry Cotton (left) had a slightly 'cupped' left wrist at the top of the backswing, while his great contemporary Ben Hogan (right) had his left hand and wrist in the same plane, or 'neutral'. Cotton used more hand action with an earlier release, and Hogan used more leg action with a later release. Much of the variation in method was attributable to the difference in ball size between Britain and the United States: whereas you could 'flick' the British ball away with a wristy action, the larger American one required a smoother approach on the forward swing. The forward swings of the two players are shown on page 55.

It has to be a player's own decision, even in the light of professional advice, which of the two methods is more economical. Certainly Cotton was physically larger than Hogan and probably stronger. Cotton 'opened the door' a lot more than Hogan and so had more closing to do, and his margin for error must have been correspondingly greater.

Open and shut cases

Professionals are interested in the position of the left hand at the top of the backswing, and in the relative position of the clubface. There are three positions here, all of which can be seen in the swings of great players:

1. The cupped left wrist and the open clubface – that is, the clubface is looking at the horizon, as is the back of the left hand and the palm of the right hand.

2. The left wrist is in plane with the back of the left hand – that is, a pencil in the wristwatch strap would lie flat along the wrist and the back of the

Left: *Fred Couples has a 'cupped' left wrist at the top of his backswing
(that is, hinged inwards), which points the clubface to the horizon and
demands a counter-clockwise rotation on the forward swing to bring the
clubface back to square. For the amateur, this can dice dangerously with the
hook shot.*

Centre: *Gordon Brand Junior, the Walker Cup player, has a 'square' or
'neutral' backswing summit, with the back of his left hand as it were at 45°
to the sky. Little compensation if any is needed to bring the clubface back
squarely to the ball. Most pros go for this line of least resistance.*

Right: *Lee Trevino has 'clawed' wrists at the top of his backswing. In
layman's language his wrists are curved upwards to the sky. This closes or
'shuts' the face but generates an opening clubface response on the forward
swing, from which he derives his fade shot.*

hand. This is called 'square' or 'neutral'. The clubface would normally
be looking up to the sky at about 45° with a medium plane swing. It would
be less with an upright swing and, with a flatter swing, even more to
the sky.

3. The 'clawed' or shut position, where the left wrist is convex (bowed
   upwards). The clubface would be 'shut' or pointing to the sky with a
   medium plane, at about 45° with an upright plane, and probably nearly
   pointing to the horizon behind the player with a flat plane.

Because there's less need to make any compensations on the forward swing
most teachers and players tend to plump for the square or neutral position
of number two on this list.

The first position (1) needs to be brought to square on the forward swing
before contact. There's not much time, but in their palmy days highly

skilful players such as Fred Couples, Ben Hogan and Henry Cotton were able to compensate very successfully and make quite a powerful physical gain. Bill Rogers had the reverse compensations to make with his shut face position (3) which brought him victory in the 1981 Open at Sandwich.

Shut-face (or clawed left wrist) actually means the club face is open to the sky, pointing to the sky. It's an awkward contradiction in terms. An open clubface 'in extremis' would point down to the ground! It must be very confusing to the layman and the less experienced amateur when he reads and hears this golfing jargon.

Lee Trevino (see picture on page 46) tends to have a clawed left wrist and thus a shut face, but I must say that most professionals, though basically 'neutral', will from time to time vary their standard positions. Some will try to change completely if they think that by so doing they will improve their skill.

Subtleties of change

I must again say that the changes they make will be so slight as to reveal very little difference to the watching public. This doesn't mean that they *feel* that the change is slight; an inch difference in plane, for example, consciously applied, would feel quite enormous. You may say, 'But that's just what the club golfer feels like.' This is the point I am trying to make: any change in a complicated habit of movement like a golf swing can take some time to establish.

The set 'nervous chain' governing that particular part which is to be changed has to be 'unlocked', turned around to activate the new movement, and then locked again. This requires not only a lot of practice but also courage – and trust that the change will be beneficial. Unfortunately you can't be absolutely sure until the change has been made and habitualized.

There's another very big 'if' about this: that is, if you do *exactly* as you are advised. I use a trick when I predict the effects of a change, first getting the patient to try the move I would like him or her to make. The initial reaction, which takes the governing nervous system by surprise, is usually quite dramatic. I get a lot of enthusiasm after this from the student and then a decline as the success is not repeated. A lot of students will battle on from there, but some others are now not so sure that this new idea will do the trick.

There's some justification for this, but what the student does not always realize is that the governing nervous chain link has suddenly 'cottoned on' to the fact that the owner is 'trying something on' – and it clamps down. Either the battle is on, or established habit continues to reign.

The memory of the brilliant result or shot is a sufficient spur for most

The top of the backswing for Snead, Aaron, Player and Crampton. In each case the shoulders have coiled 90°, with the left shoulder pointing to the ball. Optimum potential energy has been collected, but with no unnecessary strain. All these stars begin their wrist angle collection about halfway back. The elevation of the left heel, if any, is late in the backswing, though Snead employs a turn of his left foot. Also note in each case how the hands and wrists are 'adducted' to centre.

players, and they will take up the challenge. The remainder, unconvinced, will stick to the devil they know – or perhaps fall between the devil and the deep blue sea.

Hugh Baiocchi's 'think start'

I've had a lot of experience advising tour professionals. Some do not necessarily want swing changes to their swing, but are looking for mental props to support them for the next round – placebos if you like. I take great care when choosing a generalization that it is relevant to the player's swing and within the principles of my method.

Hugh Baiocchi of South Africa, who is well over six feet tall, was always under the impression that his backswing was too flat for his height. Indeed he did appear to flatten out quite a lot at the top of the backswing, but the naked eye does not take in the backswing top position, so there was no harm in encouraging him to strive for a more upright plane. It was not until I had taken a high speed movie sequence of him, however, that I realized that his backswing was already sufficiently upright. It was only on the immediate directional change that his plane flattened out or came below the backswing plane, a perfectly acceptable and indeed necessary move.

Trying to make an upright backswing would not lead to Hugh getting too high at all. It would only help to retain the desirable status quo and keep his mind off unnecessary and irrelevant aspects.

I encouraged him to 'think start' the forward swing and change direction with his hands, simply because the forward swing does start like that. This *is* the forward swing. Everything else as long as it is in the correct sequence responds to that. In fact you have not started the forward swing if you have *not* altered the course that your hands and arms have taken on the backswing.

The problem of over-analysing

There is an old Chinese story about a centipede which 'tried' to analyse which leg it used first when it walked – and it never walked again. The movements already described and those that follow are not only meant to present facts which could actually save you from over-analysing, but also to help you to recognize problems and differentiate between destructive faults and non-destructuve faults, or idiosyncracies. In other words the intention is to clear any doubt there may be about what is allowed and the alternatives to any part, or whole, of the golf swing.

The top of the backswing could be described as the moment when the clubhead has reached its optimum position before changing direction. It is said that once this position has been correctly achieved, the player has no more to do than allow the rest of the swing to take place, which suggests that from then on everything will happen as it should.

I am not so sure about the validity of that statement. While I would agree that the laws of physics should ensure perfection of response, they can do so only in the limited degree which is placed upon them by the human brain and body.

In fact, it is only in this context, which the limits of a living human being puts upon the laws of physics, that they can be used in the golf swing theory. However, if the top of the backswing is perfect there's obviously a much better chance of correct responses than if it's not.

You don't have to be perfect – but it helps

Having said that, a look at the top of the backswing of Fred Couples (see page 18 and 46) will reveal that his position doesn't exactly fit into the category of perfect. It must follow that his high level of performance comes more from a compensation on the forward swing than a response to his backswing. And it's only possible to get the best results if the player knows what the forward swing responses should be.

I don't believe that a player who does not know what the ideal forward swing should be and just allows responses to take over will have too happy a time. I believe it's still true to say that 'there's many a slip between . . . the top of the backswing, contact and finish.'

It could be said, I suppose, that it doesn't really matter what the top of the backswing is like as long as compensations are made to correct the backswing faults, but it's not as simple as that. There's less time on the forward swing to make more than one or maybe two movements to correct backswing errors. Coupled with the responsibility of making the right moves on the forward swing, or controlling the forward swing responses so that they do not 'run wild', it becomes an added and perhaps intolerable burden to also put things right there that went wrong going back.

You cannot completely copy Fred Couples. Get it right at the start and as near as possible to the top of the backswing.

Holding sway

There is a twist in the tail. Couples, like the Ryder Cup player Mark James, by dint of his 'incorrect' backswing could not only collect more potential energy that way but also be so forced into a forward swing correction that it added to his power and accuracy. There are many pros who do not keep centre on the backswing, and this must interfere with the amount of coil. They probably balance the amount of coil against the amount of sway.

The sway, incidentally, is invariably to the right. It's rare to see a professional player who has swayed to the left by the top of the backswing. This 'rightward' sway could be said to be the effect of trying to put something extra into the backswing in order to get something more out of the forward swing. There's a certain amount of truth in this because you cannot coil indefinitely. Getting the right amount of coil and then swaying a little could add something to potential energy collection, but it inevitably puts a premium on forward swing compensation. It might even help to pick up the rhythm. You might get away with a rightward sway on the backswing, but you have little chance of getting away with a leftward sway (past centre, before contact, that is) on the forward swing. The only valid leftward sway on the forward swing would be one that neutralized the amount of backswing sway.

I must emphasize that a rightward sway is not a common factor among professionals.

Les Cain, a potential tour player from Lancashire, is a regular student of mine. He was disappointed when I once took a film of his swing and pointed out that at the top of the backswing he coiled so much that his clubshaft was pointing to the right of the target (left). He thought his swing had deteriorated since I'd taken a previous sequence, and yet he was striking the ball well. The fact was that his extra turn of the shoulders was mainly the result of trying to give the shot a bit more in front of the camera. Swing fluctuation is common to all golfers, and in his case it was simply down to over-enthusiasm. Within a few shots he had his backswing well 'under control' (right), and the hanging left arm at contact (one of the effects of 'overswing') was soon moving away from his left side. Ideally, the clubshaft should never be allowed to wander across that parallel to the right of the target, since it requires complex compensations on the forward swing.

Eye on the ball?

A leftward sway at the top of the backswing is, however, a very common fault among club golfers. In the first instance it's usually the effect of trying to keep 'an eye on the ball' – the left eye.

I was once indirectly accused of wrongly teaching 'keep the left eye on the ball' by a well-known professional player from Australia. A pupil of mine had told him that I'd said he should keep his left eye on the ball. What in fact I had said was 'at the top of the backswing the left eye will be more or less in line with the back of the ball'. He had misinterpreted this, as teaching advice can so easily be misinterpreted.

There's no need at all to try to keep your eye or eyes on the ball; by that I mean looking directly at it. This only tilts the head (and so the spine) to the left, with the dire effect of tilting to the right, in an equal and opposite response on the forward swing.

In order to keep a true centre, the head should be allowed to make what feels like a slight sway to the right of a few inches when the body makes its backswing coil. This is another of those golfing paradoxes which again is almost undetectable to the observer. A sway of a foot would be clearly visible – but it would need the skills of a super pro to compensate for that.

The backswing coil

The first really good example of a backswing coil I saw was during the 1959 Walker Cup match at Muirfield. While walking to one of the tees I saw Billy Joe Patton of the American team driving off. Patton had a very rotund physique, and with the utmost respect, his trunk was just like a barrel. As he settled down in his address position, he gave the appearance of a great human cement-mixer, a head and a barrel supported by two sturdy legs. He wound up for his backswing and his round form rotated slowly on a perfect centre.

On the forward swing, still firmly held on his central axis, he derotated his large frame, which seemed to lend a tremendous surge of power to the swing of his arms. It was some consolation perhaps to see this huge man and fine golfer beaten by Scotland's Reid Jack, a player of infinitely more fragile physique.

This coiled position at the top of the backswing has its origins in the upper torso and downwards to the lower femur. I've already said (and will detail in the next chapter) that this poised position at the top will begin its uncoiling from the feet, moving upwards through knees, hips and shoulders). There should be the feeling of alliance with the ground and of an equal weight and pressure distribution between the feet. This tends to defy the argument that the weight is transferred on the backswing, despite the fact that a lot of professionals allege that they do transfer weight going back.

This is something else that is often difficult to see with the naked eye. Slow motion replays of the superstars show that they don't transfer weight but there is a change of pressure, from the inside to the ball of the left foot. This could be another common factor. A slight rightward sway is tolerable. A leftward sway is a major fault.

CHAPTER SIX

STARTING THE FORWARD DRIVE

The golf swing is a movement made with your arms. Your feet, legs, hips, trunk, shoulders and head merely support the swing of your arms, hands and club. The complex joints of the wrists also play a mainly responsive part in generating (arm) swing speed and to a certain extent this is controlled by you, the player.

When you're properly 'wound' on the backswing from above the knees, progressively through your hips to your shoulders, and there is no more available *torsion*, this spring begins to unwind. It unwinds not from the shoulders (they are wound much more, around twice as much as the hips and legs), but from the legs and hips, and this continues up to the shoulders as the swing moves forwards.

If this uncoiling fails to take place then there's a breakdown. It sort of 'strips the thread'. The knees-to-feet base gripping the ground at assembly forms the absolute basis of the backswing coil response and therefore the forward swing response. In other words, what you sow at assembly and fertilize on the backswing, you reap on the forward swing. You cannot expect to do nothing with your legs at the start and then have them do something in reply.

'Beginner's blight': spinning shoulders
While it's perfectly valid to place different emphases on the forward swing sequence, you cannot effectively change that sequence. For example, you could consciously push your legs to the left if they weren't already doing so. I suppose this could be called directly activating a response. It's not uncommon to hear some teaching pros recommending a shoulder tilt, others a hip shift to the left. I advisedly say, 'shoulder tilt'. The left shoulder tilts upwards, but at the same time the return of the shoulders is delayed.

You can't turn if you tilt; delayed shoulders are a must. Prematurely spinning shoulders are the 'beginner's blight'.

My experiences on the teaching fairway show only too often players whose shoulders, even though they reach their conventional $90°$ turn or coil on the backswing, spin prematurely. They not only do not hold the middle of the back into the target but are also turning rapidly away from it as the swing moves downwards and forwards. At the halfway point they are more

53

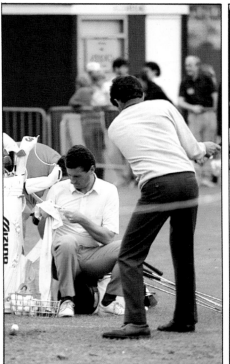

The lower body is the first area to respond to the directional change of your hands, or at least it should be. Indeed the lower body could precipitate or even anticipate your change of direction. These pictures of Spanish star Manuel Pinero show that his legs and hips are actually moving to his left (target side) before the backswing is completed.
This isn't a deliberate ploy on his part. It's just that he's so wound his upper body against his legs and feet going back that they've reached the limits of their coil, and are beginning to uncoil before he's reached the limit of his backswing. Note, incidentally, the side angle of Pinero's head to the ball during his backswing.

likely to be 45° to the left of the target line, when even to be parallel to it would be a fault.

Those victims are not the worst offenders of the 'spinning shoulders' fault, however. The most unfortunate are those players who don't make a 90° shoulder coil on the backswing, since they are already suffering from the effects of the shoulder spin even before they have started the forward swing! An 80° shoulder turn on the backswing ensures a 10° error in the forward swing which must be compounded because the shoulders, already returning to the left, can now do so with even greater ease with the 10° start

*These photographs illustrate clearly the difference in method on the Cotton
and Hogan swings. Henry's wristy style and the unflexed right leg, linked to
an early release of the wrist angle, are in marked contrast to the pronounced
leg action of the great American's forward swing, leading to a later release.*
*Cotton crossed his right arm over the left against the left arm, with the
emphasis on the wrists; Hogan delayed the crossover longer because his legs
played much more of an active role in the forward swing. The comparison at
the top of the backswing is shown on page 45. Cotton would hit against a
firm almost static left arm. Hogan's left arm was firm but active or
continuous.*

the incomplete backswing has given to them. Added to this, the lower body
(which should have been the *first* to respond) is so trapped by this upper
body predominance that it (the legs and hips) cannot respond at all.

It's very important to have a clear picture of the correct shoulder
response. The shoulders, coiled 90° on the backswing, are very likely to
uncoil rapidly if they are not held, even momentarily. If they are held, and
this may sound something of a paradox, they will in fact tilt a little, as
opposed to turning, simply because of the downward movement of the
arms. In fact if the left shoulder is tilted upwards at the top of the

backswing, that tilt will react on the arms, legs and hips. The arms will actually be compelled to change direction.

You can also get exactly the same effect by 'de-semicircling' the left knee, thus grounding the left heel. The chain reaction passes simultaneously through the hips to the shoulders and thus actually initiates the directional change of the arms. It's less likely but possible that you could change course with a right-knee flex, but you would need very well trained responses to do it this way.

Again the same things happen if the left hip is turned away to the left. Remember, it has turned to the right on the backswing, and the hands and arms responsively change direction.

It seems, no matter what you do, that you can do no wrong; but nothing could be farther from the truth. It's so easy for the inhibited and inexperienced to freeze one or more parts of the body. You have to be certain that you're allowing chain reaction, regardless of the source you're using to trigger off the directional change of the swing.

If you consciously change direction with a shoulder tilt, you must allow everything else to react; if you consciously change direction with your left foot or knee, you must allow everything else to react; if you consciously change direction with a left hip turn or return you must allow everything else to react; if you change direction, directly, with the hands and arms, you will probably have more chance this way; but again, you must allow everything else to react.

You would of course be giving all these possibilities the best possible chance to react correctly if the backswing itself were correct.

From time to time, Irv Schloss talked a lot about the disposition of the shoulders at directional change. He said, for example, 'The middle of the back, as the swing changes direction, should remain pointing towards the target, as it was at the top of the backswing. By the time the hands are halfway down, the shoulders should only be 45 degrees to the target line.'

The action films and photographs of the superstars show only too well how right he was. The fact is that the leg response to the directional change is the most efficient way of shifting the clubhead from its inert position.

Anatomy of the forward swing

The hip-shift emphasis is a slight lateral movement of the hips to the left as they uncoil. This in my opinion is pretty precarious because it could cause a rightward tilt of the spine when the spine needs to stay on the centralized axis where it began. The chain reaction of faults to this unhappy event would almost guarantee failure of the shot.

There's a school of thought which comes nearer to my own view on the hip emphasis: that is, the 'right knee flex to the left' adherents. The chain

An unhurried movement heralds the forward swing of our four 'resident' stars – Bruce Crampton, Tommy Aaron, Gary Player and Sam Snead. Remarkably, the legs are the first to respond to the change of direction, and the wrist angle, together with the 'head centering', is 'held'. The right-foot pedestal is forming: that is, heel up and moving leftwards with the pressure inside the right toe. If there's a 'misfit' here it is again with Snead, whose leg action is less dynamic and more 'bandy' than the other three, nevertheless his legs are sufficiently responsive.

reaction to this rapidly activates the hips but precludes the spinal tilt and assures the necessary transference of the weight to the left foot. But there can be nothing better than relying on responses from the assembly.

Obviously the swing unit contains two arms; some professionals will place emphasis on the activity of the right arm, others on the activity of the left. I fall into the latter school of thought, although I always bear in mind that the swing unit is the unification of the two limbs.

Left-arm emphasis keeps the leading arms (leading to target) predominant and influences the correct sequence responses and the correct path, i.e. very slightly inside to out. Right-arm emphasis can easily influence the bad path, from 'outside to in'.

There can be no doubt that the head position should be held with the left side of the face to the right side of the golf ball, and I cannot imagine an acceptable alternative to this.

It is also the case that the path of the forward swing must be slightly behind or below that of the backswing. It cannot successfully be on the same path of the backswing, and it does not take much thought to see why. The wrist angle of the backswing is delayed to approximately halfway back, and the left arm extension should take the right arm, even though the elbow joint bends downwards, away from the right side, to supply width to the backswing.

On directional change the right elbow moves into the right side because: 1 – the wrist angle is retained; 2 – the uncoiling of the body follows the knee shuffle to the left, or 3 – the knee shuffle follows the uncoiling of the body, or 4 – the simultaneous uncoiling and the knee shuffling, almost immediately pulls the right elbow into the right hip, closing any gap between the upper right arm and the torso, that was there on the backswing.

The 'handkerchief wedged into the right armpit' brigade disappeared with the hickory shaft. It was an idea in those days, before 1929, to reduce the effects of the shaft torsion. The steel shaft and the stiff graphite shaft have but little torsion – I can't say the same for the flexible graphite shaft – and so need no correction in this respect.

How much more could I say about the many differences in ideas and their application? It's been said loud and often that if your backswing is right then your forward swing will certainly be. And yet, I repeat, with respect to a fine golfer (and to Gavin Christie, his conscientious coach), Mark James has at best an unorthodox backswing which, to all intents and purposes, appears to force him into a directional change which blossoms into one of the best contacts in British golf. It thus shatters the conventional theory that the backswing must conform to certain principles to which the forward swing responds. Having said that, I'm quite convinced that if the backswing does adhere to certain principles there's a much better chance of the forward swing correctly responding, for most players, be they pro or amateur.

The John Reece story

The following extracts are taken from a letter I received in 1984 from golf writer John Reece of Bristol. I think they epitomize the inevitability of the correct sequence of the body and leg movement in support of the swing as it changes direction – if the responses are correctly based. More than this, it virtually proves that if you consciously move one area correctly it will interreact correctly on all the other areas involved.

'The accompanying photographs are sent to tell you a story of what is

By initiating his directional change
from his shoulders with a shoulder tilt,
John Reece is actually feeling a part of
the response activity of that change.
The legs will only work if they're
workable; but if you can walk on them,
you can play golf on them.

really a comeback as far as one man's golf is concerned. Let me go back a few years to the time when you gave a lecture with films at Saltford. In the middle of it you showed a sequence of me, and I remember you saying: "Why this chap is not scratch I'll never know!" I appreciated it, but only I knew the answer. I wasn't able to play enough!

'In May 1979, when I still had 18 months to go to retirement, I was stricken by a rare virus that killed all the nerve cells in my legs and most of those in my arms. It took many months to find out what was going on, during which time I saw many specialist witch doctors, and 'ologists of one sort and another, all of them experts in their subjects. At one marvellous stage I was on a neurologist's workbench at Frenchay, wired up with electrodes and needles and leads and batteries attached to me, with bats trying to fly in the windows, and sparks leaping from one terminal to another across the ceiling just like a horror movie.

'Finally, that August, Malcolm Campbell, a devoted man of medicine and common sense, assured me that provided I was patient and refused to panic he would cure me. It might take two years, but he would do it. And with nothing more than a vitamin pill!

'It was a slow business, but it worked. I had no legs worth talking about, having lost four stone in weight, and looking wasted below the waist. My original strength, which was considerable as you may recall from my boxing and training days, was completely sapped.

'Gradually, with finger-tip press-ups and yoga and a bit of running-on-the-spot, and a great deal of falling about – literally – I regained some strength, and in 1982 tottered out onto the course. I can do press-ups on my fingers, for instance, but if you put the tips of forefinger and thumb together and press them laterally, I'm beaten. That grip is gone. The area between thumb and forefinger is dead, relatively speaking. It's numb. So are my right knee and my left foot.

'As I could no longer initiate my swing from the hips because my legs would not support me, I had to adopt the 'Murray technique' of originating the entire swing from the left shoulder (or the left side of the top of the spine) and start the forward swing with a great shoulder wrench upwards.

'You can see from the more recent photographs how dead my legs are, once you know what I've told you. But the system is a cracker. I rarely use a practice swing now. One swish and I'm away, confident and repeatedly straight. It's no exaggeration to say that I'm now hitting the ball out of the centre of the clubface more consistently than ever I did when I was an aspiring able-bodied golfer. The length has diminished, of course, because I can't let everything go, but it's adequate for the job and the envy of many players. I reckon to cover 450 yards in two shots, and it's all very exciting.

'Last Wednesday I shot a 76 to win the Seniors' Open at Henbury, dropping a stroke at each of the last two holes. It was sound golf and I was very thrilled to go home to Peggy with a grin like a young puppy and say: 'I can still play.'

The photographs were all of good five-iron strokes with good results, but you may detect a certain hint of unsteadiness. Furthermore, these were hit without practice swings, and they were the first taken in 1982 when I got the weight back – most of the muscle but not the ability to use it. I'm now once again very muscular, but not very elastic. It will come, I hope. When it does I'll be down well below 8 handicap again!'

John's story graphically illustrates how demanding the game of golf is, particularly if you set your goals high. Most important, perhaps, is that you shouldn't set them higher than you know within yourself you can achieve.

There's another aspect of the story that I believe warrants serious thought. John is under the impression that his legs are inactive and, to a limited extent, he may be right about this. He certainly doesn't sprint into the forward swing like Tom Watson, but his legs *do* respond. They do not stay rigid like two sticks in the ground. In his mind, the shoulder tilt triggers the swing directional change and everything responds to that.

John certainly found his secret, albeit one forced on him by ill-health. Only time will tell whether or not this move will be permanently effective.

CHAPTER SEVEN

CONTACT

The golf swing is a whole, integrated movement, but it's quite acceptable to reduce the whole into parts to facilitate teaching and learning. 'Whole-part-whole' teaching has long been scientifically recognized as an economical way of spreading knowledge of skilled movement, and the majority of professional teachers work on this basis.

When you look at the contortions of a beginner, or even many untaught players, it becomes pretty obvious that, while they have to be taught the whole swing, there's no possible chance that they can digest this at one go. Professional players will not only be aware of the contact area or even the contact itself, but also of the prior and ensuing events.

It's all very well to set a player up correctly in the assembly position (the address) and say, 'Just swing now, you can't go wrong, everything will react to that start position.' The chance of this happening are about equal to those of sitting a child up to a piano, putting his fingers on the keyboard in the correct position and anticipating him playing a real tune.

Knowing the components

The convenience of knowing the components of the swing are more obvious when the player or would-be player knows what the responses should be to a foregoing position or movement. For example, if the reaction to a delayed wrist angle collection on the backswing is a wrist angle retention on the forward swing, and instinct says 'get the clubhead to the ball', how does that player know that the mechanics are right and the instinct wrong without being told by someone of authority or seeing it in the action of a superior player?

It's a more confident player who knows what the responses should be. Isn't it a better piano player who can read the music and hit the right notes? At the same time, it must be a better golfer who swings fluently or continuously when the ball is there than one who inches painfully through the swing in a disjointed staccato.

The whole swing is certainly a collection of parts, but which through knowledge and a lot of practice have been moulded into one complete and uninterrupted movement.

Let me reiterate. I'm talking about the responses, and how they should work. Applied movement in the contact area is not only unnecessary, but

At contact Greg Norman's shot clearly reveals the dramatic arching effect of centrifugal force. As this is only a short iron, however, his leg action hasn't been so responsive as it is with a longer club. Note how well centred he is, and how marvellously straight his left arm.

also unworkable. But pre-intended movement will work, if it is allowed to.

The contact area is a perfectly valid aspect of the swing and it is just as important to know all about this part as any other. Notice that I say contact area rather than contact position, although I am going to write about that too. In my view the contact area starts about 8 o'clock on the downswing and continues to 4 o'clock on the forward swing – that is, on the clock 'behind' you.

A high-speed movie sequence will show from six to eight positions in the sector from 8 o'clock to 4 o'clock. Each frame is $\frac{1}{64}$th of a second, and the faster the movement, the fewer the frames. A six-frame contact area takes $\frac{6}{64}$ths of a second – very fast indeed – and an eight-frame area takes $\frac{1}{8}$th of a second, which is pretty fast and certainly a high professional speed. There can be no hesitation to keep up that sort of rate, but nevertheless there is a 'contact deceleration', which I'll detail when I talk about the impact of the clubface and ball.

Analysis of pre-contact: the common factors of the pros

A number of things are taking place in this area which are common to most top players. First, from the 8 o'clock position the right heel will be coming off the ground and pointing to the left heel. This is the effect of the 'right-toe thrust', where the big right toe is 'about-to-kick' from the inside of the toe. In response, the inside of the right knee also begins to move to the left. I have previously termed this the 'right-foot pedestal'. This triggers off the whole of the right side, to begin its uncoiling round the central axis of the whole swing – that is, the spine. The right-foot pedestal, while common to the better professionals, is either rare in the club golfer or executed badly. This is due to a number of reasons but mainly because the previous movements or positions have not formed the correct basis for the correct responses. It's trite, perhaps, but a good move brings on another good move and a bad move brings on another bad one.

Second, the left side, in response to the uncoiling right side, is winding around that central axis. Some teachers describe this as 'the left side getting out of the way', or words to that effect. As long as the meaning is conveyed to the student, the actual terminology is unimportant.

Clamping the left heel to the ground is common to many pros on or even before directional change. But so many very good players (Joyce Wethered, Bobby Jones and George Archer among them) lead a string of stars who actually contact the ball with the left heel off the ground, that it's doubtful whether the 'clamp downers' can be slotted into the common factor pigeon-hole.

The left heel return to the ground, if it ever comes off the ground on the backswing, certainly follows a more logical, secure and economical pattern.

I can remember Henry Cotton advocating keeping the left heel up until after contact to cure a hook, and it worked.

Some professional players delay the uncoiling by what's known as *sliding the hips*. Byron Nelson was the most famous 'hip slider', but it's safe to say that this somewhat doubtful practice is now going out of fashion, for it always carries with it the danger of swaying off-centre. Strangely enough, that sway is more likely to be off-centre to the right than to the left. The lateral thrust of the left hip tends to tilt the spine to the right. The head weight increases the tilt.

Third, the top stars have in common the retention of the wrist angle they previously collected either on the backswing or on the change of direction. This leaves the clubhead tracking well behind the hands, a condition to which many club golfers find it difficult to subscribe. They are constant victims of the instinctive urge to 'get the clubhead to the ball'.

Fourth, the left side of the face, the left cheek, will be held to the right side of the ball by so many top pros that it can safely be called another of their common factors. I have noticed a few of the younger set of playing professionals who seem to rotate their heads rather earlier. But one wonders whether, in fact, this is the development of a fault.

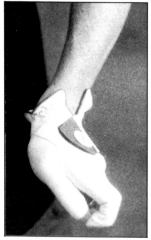 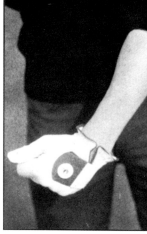 

The wrists on contact

There are two ways of releasing the wrists too early – by 'hingeing' and by 'rotation'. The hinge (above left) is a right-angled flex at the back of the left wrist and the front of the right wrist to the right. Hingeing might well be described as flipping or flicking. Also called hyper-extension, it's essentially a scooping action best avoided rather than cultivated in the swing.
Rotation (above centre, above right, opposite left) is a rather more refined wrist action, where the right wrist gradually rotates over the left in a counter-clockwise direction, both flowing continuously to target. Doing this

Fifth, by 8 o'clock the shoulders are nearly parallel to the target line, but tilted. The left shoulder is up and the right shoulder is down. This is so much the case with all the star professionals as to merit the designation of 'common factor'. The only differences are those of degree. Some have more tilt than others and some not quite so near to the parallel as others.

Timing the release

It's said that the handicap golfers at this stage can be very different from their golfing idols, and the higher the handicap the greater the chasm between those players and the stars.

If their right heels are not pinned to the ground, they will be twisting grotesquely to the left and severely diverting the swing path, to mention only one outcome. Their left sides rarely glide smoothly around the spinal axis. For the most part they don't coil or uncoil at all and consequently impede the fluidity of the right side.

That's probably why the shoulders are so advanced at this stage in the

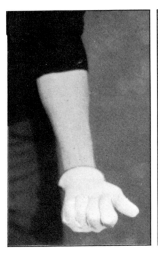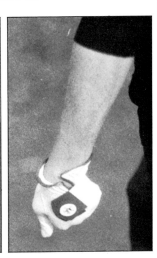

excessively or too early in the forward swing isn't only effectively releasing too soon but also courting a vicious hook.

Retention of the wrist angle, however, with the wrists still protruding to the target away from the swing centre is termed flexion or 'abduction' (above centre) and is the most desirable of the options. The secret, if there is one, lies in trying to balance the qualities of the two approaches, and releasing the wrists neither too early nor too late, coupled with the counter-clockwise rotation.

Arching (above right) is the contact effect of centrifugal force on the wrists.

less skilled and why too, the wrist angle has already been dissipated, even before the 8 o'clock position, to say nothing of the impossibility of keeping centred through all this maze of errors.

The top players are adept at releasing late in the contact area. This means quite simply that they release their wrist angle collection at a point when the hands are past the ball position *before* the clubface has made contact with the ball.

This has the desirable effect of starting the ball flight low and then gradually soaring until the peak is reached. Obviously this will give the ball a longer carry in the air than a shot that reached its peak very rapidly. Some pros actually hold the wrist angle until the hands are past the left foot; Lee Trevino comes to mind immediately as an outstanding example of this. Others will release with their hands just past the ball. But it must be remembered that release is variable and depends on the type of shot required. Releasing too late will produce too low a shot and probably one that also veers to the right.

Not releasing at all simply means blocking out the clubface to the right so that it twists the ball to the right. It's also possible with a wood to hit the ball too high by leading downwards with the hands and so plunging the face of the club down into the ground, thus contacting the ball with the top of the face. Sometimes this can be deep enough to make contact with the top of the inset. But the hands leading too much is in this case almost always caused by loss of centre to the left rather than too long a wrist angle retention. If, for example, the clubhead is still trailing when the hands reach 6 o'clock, which is quite desirable, the clubhead should be well on its way past the hands before they have reached 5 o'clock. In other words the clubshaft is fully loaded at 8 o'clock, but by 4 o'clock it should be completely unloaded. My photos of Seve Ballesteros on page 67 demonstrate this perfectly.

Hitting 'down' and hitting 'up'

A lot of teachers advise different approaches to the contact area and the contact itself. With iron clubs they recommend hitting down onto the ball, while with the woods they go for hitting up to the ball, especially with the driver. This particular view is sound, but isn't it stating the obvious?

If you think about it, the ball placement in relation to the stance actually does the job for you. From a wedge to a seven-iron, the ball should be placed opposite the centre of the feet, measuring this from between the heels, and progressing a couple of inches with the six, five, four, three, two, and one irons towards the left foot.

Depending on individual tolerances, it will be seen that for most of the irons the ball will be contacted at the lowest point in the swing circle and will thus produce a 'downward' contact. The longer irons will be contacted very early on the upward curve of the circle but certainly not enough to partially top or 'thin' it. The fairway woods should occupy a similar left of centre position to the two and one-iron – not quite left heel, which would lend itself to a 'sweeping' as opposed to a 'squeezing' contact. A teed-up ball for a driver or a two-wood, even a three-wood, is automatically 'swept up' when it is positioned opposite the left heel.

I make no apologies for repetition here. The ball should never be positioned further left than the left heel. The curve of the circle, and so the clubhead, would be running out of the stratum of the ball beyond that safety mark.

Exceptions to the ball placement from the centre to the left heel are for special shots, when the ball is placed to the right of centre for very 'descending' blows, and opposite the left toe for 'ascending' contact. Indeed some club golfers can gain a few yards by this 'left-toe, high-tee'

Seve Ballesteros demonstrates the effects of centrifugal arching and rotation of the arms, wrists and hands as a unit. Before contact the shaft is 'loaded' – you still have it. After contact it's 'unloaded'. Metaphorically, you have 'thrown it away'.

trick, but they invariably seem to fall apart when they have to play a shot that is not teed up. In other words too much hitting up can make it more difficult to hit down, and one way or another, but certainly wrongly, too many players are hitting at the ball rather than swinging through.

Assembly and contact: static v dynamic

The contact position is so often equated with the assembly position that it's not surprising so many players fall into the trap of trying to make them exactly the same.

In the first place the assembly is a static position, while the contact is dynamic. It's most important to keep the contact dynamic, fluid or continuous even though it may not feel like the assembly by so doing. It doesn't have to feel like the assembly, because the contact is totally different from it.

In the second place the continuity of contact is essential because of the

GIVING IT A BIT LESS

I doubt there's ever been a golfer who at some time hasn't succumbed to the temptation to 'give it a bit more' – but the net result is nearly always a bit less. The real bargain, of course, is a bit less to get a bit more. The answer to more length lies in improved control and better timing, not in simply increasing the physical effort. A fair golfer who is struggling for length may well find that if he sacrifices swing power for more rhythm and control the product is a gain in yardage as well as in accuracy.

Macdonald Smith, star of the 1920s and a Carnoustie emigrant to the United States, was once asked by a golfing reporter how he could get the extra yards over his 'normal' length drives, seemingly at will, 'I just take it a wee bit easier, laddie,' he replied.

Applied acceleration is no less than unnecessary interference with a physical law. It's not difficult to imagine what happens to a pendulum when you try and hasten its 'natural' acceleration; you get the very opposite of what you intended, namely loss of control and power. According to Irv Schloss, this tendency to do more than the job demands was a symptom of what he called the 'English disease' in golf, the temptation to 'use a sledge-hammer to crack a walnut'.

spontaneous deceleration which takes place when the clubface is breaking through the resistance of the ball and the build up of resistance in the whole of the left side of the body. If the continuity of the swing breaks down on contact deceleration, that deceleration is compounded and further acceleration is not usefully possible.

A cold look at all the static differences between impact and address shows quite a catalogue of disparity. By static differences I mean the positional variations between a photographically frozen view of the contact and that of the assembly, which of course by-passes the dynamic difference. Here I am comparing experts.

The feet are very different. The right foot is firmly based at assembly, and at impact the heel is off the ground. The left foot is taking pressure inside the shoe at assembly but at impact, if the heel has returned to the ground, the weight and pressure will be transferred to the outside of the shoe round to the heel – with the exception of those players who don't return the heel until *after* contact.

The same applies to the knees. Both knees are flexed a little towards the ball and a little towards each other at address, but at impact they're both flexed towards the left to varying degrees. The right knee is bending,

The contacts of Snead, Crampton, Aaron and Player are all a combination of hands leading the clubhead, wrists arching and the forearms rotating simultaneously. All, of course, have left-wrist abduction. The legs are sprinting now while the hips rapidly 'derotate', with the shoulders (slowly in relative terms) moving back into parallel. Only the flow, the centering and the finger pressure will be felt as the clubface temporarily decelerates on impact with the ball, then breaks through this split-second setback to accelerate spontaneously into the follow through. It's too late to change your mind here; you have to let fly. For at least 6 inches through the ball, however, the clubhead must track straight along the target line.

parallel to the target line towards the left knee which is 'de-semicircling' around to the left, on its way to winding the left leg to extension or straight.

At assembly the hips may be slightly turned to the left, in opposition to the parallel shoulders, but the belt buckle will be facing the golf ball. By contact the hips will be so rotated that the belt buckle will be just about facing the target; this is an appreciable difference. Although moderately tilted at assembly, the shoulders are noticeably tilted at contact. The left shoulder is high, the right shoulder is low.

The arms at assembly are extended with the right elbow flexed in a little towards the left elbow; at contact the left arm extension is increased and the right elbow is flexed even more in towards the left elbow. The wrists and hands, sunk slightly at the start, are arched at contact by the effects of the reaction of centrifugal force. If the hands are arched at assembly, centrifugal force will arch them even more at contact and counter clockwise rotation will combine with the abduction of the wrists and hands.

The shaft flex is also different at impact than it was at address. Centrifugal force will bend it so that the head is pulled in towards the player. The shaft bend is outwards, towards the ball.

Fuzzy Zoeller, the extrovert American, is an unwitting but perfect example of the centrifugal effect on the shaft of a golf club at contact. At address he holds his clubface well *outside* the ball (that is, away from him), yet it comes back with the clubface dead centre on the ball. I asked him about this, but he said he didn't really do it consciously.

Continuity on contact

One of the dangers of trying to make an assembly-shaped contact is that everything then becomes static when it should be fluid. The old adage that it's better to have two feet on the ground doesn't apply when you should be allowing the golf swing to regain acceleration through impact. The golf ball shouldn't be an immovable object: the swing should be an irresistible force.

It's a mistake to think that because the hands are leading the clubface as they move past the ball they will be ahead at contact. The 'arching' effect of centrifugal force does a rapid 'straightening job' on the left arm, wrists and shaft, despite that outward flexing of the shaft.

Good contact has everything to do with good coordination between eyes and hands as they bring the club squarely into the back of the ball along that imaginary, broad, 12-inch line. With good centering it's held less than 1000th of a second longer, but it sends it that much further.

Ideally the clubface should be turning tightly into the ball at contact, and by 4 o'clock, if not earlier, it should be facing directly at right-angles to the target line. This is in response to rotation taking over from arching, which took over from wrist angle retention.

The left side of the face should still be held just to the right side of the ball at contact and the ball position after contact and at least the 4 o'clock limit of the contact area. In fact I shall point out in the next chapter that for the best results the centering should hold well beyond the contact area.

Most professionals are in agreement that good contact is the effect of good responses to previous movement and good assembly, and that it has far more to do with intentions than application.

CHAPTER EIGHT

COMPLETING THE SWING

Irv Schloss was always very keen on what he called 'rightward discipline'. By this he meant taking a path through the contact area which could be called *inside-to-out* – from inside past the right foot to outside past the left foot. At the same time he still advocated that 12-inch straight line through the ball. The tendency for most students is to exaggerate this to be sure of doing it.

The inside path, already established as necessary by the compensation of the uncoiling right side on the forward swing before contact, must take an outside path as it progresses. It's the *amount* of outside path than can become a stumbling 'block-out' when it is overdone.

It may seem a bit of a paradox to talk at the same time about a straight line through contact and an inside-to-out path. But the curve of the arc which goes gradually 'in' on the backswing and even more 'in' on the early part of the forward swing, goes minimally out again through contact, before going in again. You could easily ask the question, 'when is a straight line not a straight line? – and get the answer, 'when it travels like the golf clubhead through the 12-inch contact area which contains the ball'. Tony Jacklin advocates even more of an inside-to-out path through contact than Irv Schloss did, but this is probably more to do with feel than fact.

Applied 'fade' and 'draw'

An accurately executed inside-to-out path with the minimal outward direction has the desirable effect of starting the ball to the right of target and, coupled with the right amount of counter-clock rotation of the hands, which applies a leftward spin to the ball, brings it back into target. It's a highly skilful and effective way of applying a 'soft draw' to the ball, thus stealing a few more yards from the fairway.

There is another technique for doing this, one of which the Swedish tour player Peter Dahlberg is an expert. He stands with his feet aiming to the right (the degree depends on how much he wants to start the ball to the right) and holds the face of the club to the target. His swing path follows the line of his feet and thus starts the ball to the right on the initial thrust before the 'leftward' spin, which the square and then the rotating clubface imparts, brings it back to target.

Peter fades a shot with the stance lined to the left of target and the clubface square to target. The initial thrust takes the ball left and this time the spin, which is 'rightward', brings the ball back to target from the left.

The important thing to remember about the applied fade and draw is the swing path: it must follow the alignment of the feet. 'Inside-to-out' for the draw, 'outside-to-in' for the fade.

Irv Schloss always looked on the soft draw, played with the feet square to the target line and the cultivated 'rightward discipline', as the best stock shot. 'It's nearly impossible to guarantee or certainly set up a deliberately straight shot', he would say, and I am one of many who share this view.

Hitting 'straight'

I know of many other pros who can more successfully 'bend' a shot one way or another, and they too find it much easier to teach a curved flight. Even if the intended 'soft draw' blossoms into a straight shot, as it could do occasionally if the feet are aiming square, it must go straight to target, who can grumble about that?

If the outside path is so minimal that it barely exists, so then it is just as 'imaginary' but equally valid to feel a straight path through and beyond contact. This, too, must gradually follow the uncoiling of the body and travel progressively 'inside'. How much inside is, for the most part, dependent on the plane of the swing and therefore on the length and the lie of the club you are using, your physique (notably your height), and tolerances. You'll be flatter with your driver than with your wedge, but there should be no need to deliberate about that: let the club do it for you. It will, if the sole of the club is properly grounded in each case; that means with the toe very slightly elevated, by no more than would allow a large coin to be placed horizontally under it.

A 'feel' for swing

By the time the swing has reached this 'advanced' stage the speed is so relatively high (from contact to the swing finish is the fastest part of the swing, and the player is or should be under the influence of this speed) that the controls are now well into the realms of response, and beyond any measure of controlled application.

An overall 'feel pattern' is useful here. My father always used to say about contact-to-swing finish that you should *feel* as though you're going to hook the ball but in fact it goes straight. I must confess it took me a few years for the wisdom of this to seep through to me.

The swing path very much gives the feel of going round; but not too abruptly. There's an unfortunate aversion to this by handicap golfers who erroneously think that this is 'coming across it'. One of my pupils watched Sandy Lyle winning the Open at Sandwich in 1985. 'I didn't like his swing

PLANE CHECK ON THE FORWARD SWING

This is simply the reverse of that on the backswing (in Newnes All-Colour Guide to Golf*). Although only a practice ground exercise it's good for conveying the feel of the correct plane position. The drill, demonstrated here by the Ghanaian champion Joseph Awuku, is as follows. Swing to 3 o'clock on the forward swing and stop there (left); switch your stance, now normally parallel to the target line, to be at right-angles to the target line, while still holding the 3 o'clock position (centre). You're now facing your target. Lower the club from the waist until it's properly grounded (right). If your plane is still 'intact', when the club is grounded it should be in a similar position in relation to your feet as it was at the assembly.*

If, when the club is grounded, it's a long way to the left of this original position, the plane has flattened too much; in other words, it has gone too much 'inside' to the left. If it's grounded well to the right of its original position then the plane has been too upright, or it has taken too much of an outside path away from the right foot. Either way the 'plane barrier' has been broken.

– he came across the ball,' she said. 'Not really,' I explained. 'That was your eye-view of his swing plane, which would be more apparent if you were watching from an angle in front of him but looking at the back of him,' which of course she was. The swing looks very 'round' from that angle, but very straight when viewed frontally.

Seeing too much of the ball

So many players see more of the flight of the ball than is necessary, even for a successful reading of the feedback. They look too soon at the flying ball and deprive themselves of the advantages of proper centering.

Centering on the forward swing is controlled mainly by the head position, which in turn effects the movements of the spine and the backswing responses to the winding or torsion of the body around it. In a sense the gradual straightening of the left leg on the forward swing is multi-purpose. One of its functions is to hold the uncoiling trunk in to the centre, with the help of the head centering, similar to the way the right leg and head positioning hold the coiling body in to centre on the backswing. 'Head down', by the way, has nothing to do with centering.

The hip rotation or derotation to the left is complete only when the left leg has extended or straightened. The weight from the right foot has all been shed to the outside of the left foot from the toe to the heel. This is best felt when the swing centre and plane have been properly retained.

So, centering on the forward swing is controlled mainly by the head position. The left side of the face should be held just to the right side of the ball position until the ball has gone, but 'until the right shoulder touches the chin' is even better. This is coupled with the gradual de-semicircling of the left knee and the flexing of the right knee towards it. While finalizing the hip rotation, derotation or left side clearance (to quote a few 'teaching variations'), this also has the further effect of supplying resistance to the swing and aiding continuity.

The 'left leg' debate

The 'straightened left leg' is controversial among the pros, both playing and teaching, as is the 'retained flexed left knee'. Certainly you should not straighten the left leg *before* contact.

I remember the USPGA coaches at the first all-American PGA school in Florida all being in favour of the final straightening of the left leg. Then along came one of the students, a young professional, brandishing a photograph of Jack Nicklaus taken at the end of his swing and showing the left knee still flexed. 'What about this then?' challenged the dissident to the platform.

It might have been Dr Gary Wiren, then the educational director of the USPGA, who answered that this was Nicklaus exercising his poetic and indeed professional licence to make (most certainly for very good reasons) a little deviation.

Breaking the rules

I believe that while for the most part the superstars will stay within the limits of their common factors, they have such finely tuned skills that they can improvize almost at will. They can create special shots that demand movements which break the rules. The great thing about these improvized

Greg Norman's swing finish has all the common factors of Snead and his friends (see page 77), and all the great names of golf from Vardon to Ballesteros (see page 79). Responsive and spontaneous they may be, but only because everything that went before was absolutely right.

shots is that you can think up your own. If they're effective then they are obviously acceptable, but it's still advisable to stay within the bounds of a method as much as possible.

The extension of the arms, once the swing has broken through the impact resistance, is not all that difficult if the thoughts and intentions are right. Most professionals have both arms fully extended to around 3 o'clock. The differences are only at the stages when the left arm begins to 'give' at the elbow. Some go on to even 1 o'clock, while others begin to fold by 3 o'clock. The majority of strong pro players keep their left-arm radius until around the 2 o'clock mark.

For a number of very different reasons the club golfer's radius has gone on or too soon after contact – sometimes even before it.

The pros try to keep the ball down somewhat, so there is no need to make the flipping action or 'flick' which follows the club golfer's pre-intention of getting the ball into the air. This has nothing to do with hitting the ball on the upward swing, or arc, as with a driver; this is simply the effect of ball positioning at assembly.

The fear of not getting the ball airborne makes the handicap player prone to the hingeing illustrated on page 64. This happens in the contact area and in consequence the early collapse of the left arm at the elbow follows this hingeing almost immediately and this frustrates any possibility of post-contact extension. I have seen players try to add extension to collapse, obviously completely ineffectively. I expect all of us have seen the player who seems to stop his swing around the 3 o'clock position, then suddenly burst into a new movement which at best can only be a contribution to vanity and at worst is utterly pointless.

The unbroken and abducted left wrist through contact and beyond is a feature of all the best players ever. My sequence of Gary Player's swing on page 142 is a vivid example of this. The long retention of the wrist angle which brings the hands beyond the ball before the clubface meets the ball, the gradual counter-clock rotation of the hands and arms (sometimes described – erroneously in my opinion – as pronation) presents an involved movement which must be practised long and hard before expertise is achieved. Even then, it would amount to very little without correct centering and plane.

Formulas for long hitting

Long hitting is a combination of ideals. Of paramount importance is contact with the centre of the clubface which, if the ball is to go to target, must also be square to that target. Second, the clubface must be held into the ball for the longest possible time; not more than a tiny fraction of a second but, if it's anything less, the contact will be glancing and the ball

Snead, Aaron, Player and Crampton: once again the swing orbits round the (now reversing) coil of the body, which is winding round the spine. There's no hand brake, no foot brake. The swing must be allowed to crash to a finish – with the expert still balanced comfortably in the driving seat and firmly in control.

won't fly so far. Third, correct clubhead speed: if the ball is hit off-centre and struck a glancing blow all the clubhead speed in the world will be to no avail. How can these ideals be achieved? It would be good to say, 'quite easily', but after much practice with the right formula it gets easier.

Part of that formula is the unbroken left-arm radius. By that I mean from hand to shoulder as a unit with the delayed release and the gradual counter clock rotation, coupled with the spinal centering via the head control, plane retention and right side flow. This will bring centre contact which clings to the ball, and you'll feel it through the shaft vibration; the longest shot you ever made will feel strangely effortless.

This formula can be reduced to something like the following. Keep the left cheek just to the right side of the golf ball position until the right shoulder touches the chin. You will feel that you are looking down there twice as long as you should. Allow the swing to orbit round the body coil (or uncoil as it could be called in this case) and as you are looking down there you might casually glance at your right knee as it flexes past your chin progressively towards the left knee. You do not need to add anything else in the way of assistance to the clubhead to get through the ball, nor inhibit it. Simply, let it swing *continuously* as the body joins in the flow round its centre.

You should feel the left side, from the foot right up to the shoulder, winding around the spine. The hips will be well in advance of the shoulders, which will turn more or less to completion when the right shoulder points to the ball position, much the same as the left shoulder did on the backswing. The hips, which normally only seemed to be facing the target, now certainly will be!

Repetition of this movement in part only must simplify its inclusion into the whole swing shape. Once it becomes habit, it will produce a lot of results for the minimal expense of energy.

Centering the head position

For the easiest head centering we have to go back to the assembly. A lot of players tilt the head to the right here. Frankly, I've found that it's much easier to 'hold' a centre both on the backswing and (in particular) the forward swing when the face is held directly down to the ball with the left cheek moving only fractionally to the right of the ball as the swing changes direction – and until that right shoulder is brought to the chin at the latest. It will be possible to modify this as the skill improves.

It's not a good policy to glue the head into position until the end of the swing. It's a common enough factor of the superstars that they are looking at the flight of the golf ball, or certainly the last part of it, for the handicap players to safely adopt that factor in their own swings.

If there is a 'secret' to the swing I believe it lies in this segment, having said that this segment is dependent on the assembly and the backswing. You cannot sacrifice everything else about a golf swing for one section of it, even when that section contains the vital elements. The real secret is knowing what these are and sowing the right seeds to produce them.

Again, I've never yet seen a good golfer with a bad assembly; I have seen good players with good assemblies and not wonderful backswings. But through contact the assembly seeds have choked out the backswing weeds and the miracle then blossoms.

Separating the segments: the spiral

If you are not looking for it, you probably won't see it, I'm referring in this

The Ballesteros spiral, upwards beyond contact and clearly seen from this angle, kills the myth of the 'keep down throughout' theory. This is the only way to maintain swing speed around the swing centre.

case to the spiral of the body from around the three o'clock position to the finish of the swing. Unless you're looking you won't see any other swing segment either. Even if you are looking there are some parts you will not see anyway. They are either too fast or merely deceptive. The high finish before the 'maypole' dissipation of energy is one of the segments impossible to see with the naked eye. So is the top of the backswing: the eyes become confused between the lower body response and the actual swing pause before directional change.

Seve Ballesteros is the best example of the spiral (see page 79), because his is so pronounced. Most spectators miss this because they are diverted by the flight of the golf ball, which they find magnetic – understandably in a competitive situation.

The completion of the extension of the left leg, combined with the roll onto the toe of the right foot, winds the body upwards and around the spine. The professionals allow this to happen. The handicap golfer is so intent on 'staying down' that the natural spiral is inhibited or is made too early, albeit unwittingly. This latter then heralds that good intention which paves the way to the nether regions: 'Next time: I'll stay down.'

You can't just add the spiral to the swing: it must flow spontaneously to ensure the continuity of the swing. The feet, legs and hips are responsible for the spiralling and they in turn are reacting in anticipation of and in response to the acceleration of the arms which, at that stage, are reaching their peak speed. The rotation of the head also helps the swing continuity and as such is involved with the spiral.

The flow of the swing should be interrupted only when the kinetic energy is dissipated. Otherwise there is an inevitable premature braking which throws the body out of sequence, centre and balance.

The body should have come to its ultimate position before the hands have taken the arms through the full circle. They would then be 'maypoling' round the spine until the kinetic energy ran out. With a lot of pro players this brings the clubshaft low across the neck and shoulders, and to the non-expert analyser it looks as though the swing has flattened out considerably. But the eyes have missed it.

Bernhard Langer's swing, for example, is so swift that the watching public are deceived into believing that his swing flattens out after contact – so much so that he has accidentally provoked a new 'school' of thought. But Langer, like the rest of his colleagues in the golfing firmament, has a high maximum finish and a 'low maypole'.

A high maypole, a low maypole, or a 'Palmer reverse maypole' – I have seen Ballesteros produce all three during a serious golf game.

I know a few teachers who actually start their pupils off by teaching them the end of the swing first, and there's a lot to be said for this. It's just as logical as building a landing strip for aircraft before the aircraft have to land, the maypole finish being the landing strip in the golf swing. I've found when I experimented with this that pupils were more able to equate the preparation and the backswing with the whole movement better than when they were left in the dark before the final objective was revealed.

For the most part, however, I still prefer to start at the beginning. The trouble with starting at the end of the swing is convincing students that it really matters what happens there.

CHAPTER NINE

THE ELEMENTS OF MOTION

Both professionals and handicap players suffer variations of form; and while the pros experience less fluctuation than the club golfers, it should be remembered that the slightest lapse on their part can be infinitely more costly than, say, a nasty bout of slicing by the weekend pleasure player.

The trouble with professionals is that they too derive enjoyment from playing golf, so their lapses not only herald financial losses but also deprive them of the enjoyment of playing well.

Why is it possible to play good shots one day and not the next? It's a question I've been asked by almost every student I've ever taught.

Human weakness means simply that in any kinetic skill, error is at some stage inevitable. It's just not possible to make a complicated movement for any length of time without making a mistake. Then, if the error is not immediately identified and corrected, it will tend to repeat itself and become a bad habit. The resultant loss of form then threatens to become permanent.

Pressure: physical or psychological?

It's generally thought that the pressures in golf are almost entirely mental. But are they? It is, for example, far more pleasant to play in the warm sunshine of a Florida winter than it is in a howling gale and a November downpour on a Scottish links. Such a setting would be detrimental to almost any player's concentration and rhythm.

Physical injury, even though it be only a cut finger, can make normal shot production virtually impossible, though it must be said that injury or disability hasn't been allowed to get in the way of quite a number of very determined professionals. It's worth reminding readers of the wonderful feat of Jim Ferrier, the Australian who despite two broken thumbs won an American major in the 1960s, and in more recent times Calvin Peete achieved success after a broken left arm was badly and permanently set in an unnatural bow.

Of course it needs an extraordinary mental effort to overcome extraordinary physical disabilities. But I'm not so sure that the adjustments needed for major disabilities are any greater than, if as difficult as, the corrections needed to counteract the constant changing of the human body.

We hear only of the top names making a change in their swings, and I have to smile a little when I hear about such events. A grip change or a plane change by some golfing legend is happening to every player in both the major and minor circuits of professional golf every day. They are merely the adjustments or corrections necessary to combat human variations and evolution, in order to keep the essence of the golf swing the same or nearly the same as before.

Why is the pro so much better than the club golfer?

I realize I have yet to answer the question of why the pros have less fluctuations than the handicap players. There are, quite literally, more than a dozen areas where the pros are above average, more than a dozen key areas to analyse. The first is *physique*, though not necessarily related to sheer size. Gary Player, for example, is strong but not nearly as large as Andy Bean. Nevertheless, as in many ball games, a 'good big 'un' will tend to outhit a 'good little 'un'. The second is *aiming ability*, where good eyesight is an obvious asset, whether natural or corrected. A third is *speed* of movement, but without effort or strain. In fact it's noticeable that most professional tour players achieve maximum effect with the minimum expenditure of energy. Nevertheless they can never be accused of 'going soft' on the big ones, and they can be working hard at one aspect of their game without it being obvious.

A fourth difference is obviously in *accuracy*, which demands a precise attention to detail in the static, and the ability to repeat a swing shape that is well centered. *Economy of movement* is another quality which can elude the club golfer, and conserve vital energy. The not-so-good player will be seen to be all over the place, against the precise, almost restrained movement of the expert. Six, there is the exertion of *muscular power* over the short period of time it takes to swing, i.e. the dynamic part of it. This is tied up with strength, speed and economy of movement, and amounts to making the optimum use of that time – less than two seconds of it for the pro swing.

Another aspect of that is muscular strength exerted in a single phase of the action – in other words the strength imparted by the whole body for accurate change of direction, the strength imparted by the hands and arms through the contact area and the consequent strength of the rest of the body to maintain position. *Hand-eye coordination* is essential for impact perfection as in all ball sports, and in golf it must be linked to club/ball coordination because of the relatively small contact area. With the less skilled player a good contact happens with nothing like the frequency the pros enjoy; intelligent practice improves coordination.

Hand-wrist-arm coordination, is obviously linked with eyes, club-head and ball coordination but involves the range of shots in which these

The American 'Mini Ryder Cup' player David Glenz is probably the player with the smoothest tempo I've ever seen, and yet it exudes power. He allows himself all the qualities of potential and kinetic energy – space, time, weight, force and flow (see page 86).

factors predominate – singly for short and together for the medium and long shots. There should be a conscious distribution of their use as opposed to a spontaneous one. In other words the hands and arms are intentionally used for the medium and long shots while the hands are intentionally used for the short shots.

Good **balance** is important, too, beginning its life in the static part of the swing and related to stance, pressure and weight distribution, posture and placement of arms in relation to the body. Even a faulty grip can ultimately affect the balance when the body overreacts in an attempt to correct. Centering, coiling, extension, plane, winding and speed are all factors which influence balance. The professional player knows his personal limitations in respect of these, or at worst 'senses' them, by instinct or experience, or both.

Agility is yet another, though not so vital factor, related to the speed a player moves both on his way round the course and, much more importantly, during his actual swing. The measure of agility varies from pro to pro but compared to the average golfer it wouldn't be unkind to say that the typical pro is rather more agile and supple. Age is obviously a factor which affects agility, but not the only one. Tom Watson is perhaps the most agile superstar I have ever seen – and Bobby Locke perhaps the least. Nevertheless Locke had a beautifully smooth if very idiosyncratic action.

Another necessary ingredient to enhance any kinetic skill is **rhythm**. Even a casual observer of the competitors on the practice ground at any major pro tournament cannot help being impressed by the rhythms of all the players. I say rhythms in the plural because they all have their personal tempos, even if they are all unhurried, effortless and repetitive. **Dexterity** is an aspect of feel, particularly in the fingers and hands. The control of the grip pressures, for example, has more to do with finger pressures than grabbing fiercely with the whole of the hands and fingers. Far too many weekend golfers grip either too lightly or too tightly.

The need for **stamina** is obvious: it is not possible to play 36 holes of golf a day for two successive days at a professional level without being endowed with a high level of physical and psychological endurance. **Adaptability**, is required, too, being able to perform just the same under adverse conditions, known or unexpected, and coping with external and internal pressures, from crowds to nasty weather to unpleasant opponents.

The **ability to practise** is also self-explanatory. I've said before that spaced practice is good general practice, while mass practice is good for swing fault correction. The lucky ones among you actually enjoy practising. A common professional weakness is lack of courage to practise weaknesses to turn them into strengths, especially when spectators are around. Some pros will wisely retire to a quiet spot to overcome their weaker shots. However, I'm very much in favour of practising the easy shots (easy for the player concerned). It does help swing repetition.

After all these aspects I will rate **kinesthetic sense** as the most important quality, the one which probably separates the pro from those amateur players who have handicaps from four upwards. The word means, broadly speaking, an inward sense of the 'feel' of the muscular and anatomical movements involved in the golf swing, or for that matter in any other skilful movement, part or whole. 'Feel' means just what it says. A lot

LEFT-HANDED PRACTICE

There are a few remarkable players who are just as good left-handed as right-handed. Johnny Bulla, a former US tour pro, was completely ambidextrous, playing just as well left-handed as right-handed. The amazing thing was that he could take a right-hand club, turn it over, toe downwards and hit perfect left-handed shots with it. The late D. C. Jones, who was the pro at North Manchester in England, was another brilliant player either left- or right-handed. I remember a great friend of mine, former Scottish Professional Champion Hamish 'Jimmy' Ballingall, regularly practising left-handed shots, although he was normally right-handed. In my opinion this is a useful form of practice, in regular but small doses.

This is, perhaps, an appropriate place to apologize to (and sympathize with) the left-handers among my readers. I hope you'll forgive the automatic use of the right-handed model in all my examples, for they are in a large majority (more so than in any other ball contact sport) and in any case it would be totally impracticable to have on each occasion covered the left-handed variation in the text.

of players, professionals as well as club golfers, think of it in some sort of mystical terms, but it can be acquired. First of all it is necessary to know the mechanics of the movement and then, with the help of slow swing practice, feel this mechanism at work. Using a weighted wooden club is excellent for developing a keener 'kinesthetic' sense, and so is playing shots blindfolded.

No miracles, but . . .

In the search for a secret we've probably unearthed many secrets, if indeed they could be called secrets. I'm more inclined to call them guidelines, pointers, keys or cues, if you like. But here and now I can assure my readers that there's no such phenomenon as a 'magic move' which overnight would transform an 18-handicap player to a scratch player. Nevertheless, I do think it's possible to unearth one tiny scrap of information which could completely alter the whole movement of a player for the better.

It's quite some time since I latched onto the real concept of 'plane', for example, but once I did it seemed to me that this alone made me feel for the first time that my game was, at least in appearance, truly professional. It was the missing link which made more sense of everything that I knew went on in my golf swing from a playing point of view and it increased, if it did not perfect, my knowledge of a golf swing from a teacher's point of view.

There is plenty for every player to study and copy in the swing of Tom Watson, one of the most masterful of all the great Americans:
Left: *He displays space even at assembly. His posture is up and the clubhead is out, away from his feet. At the same time his upper arms are 'grooved' near his body. He will take time to set himself before starting back.*
Right: *At the top of his backswing he still uses the optimum amount of space and time (within the safe limits of his agility and strength) to change direction successfully.*

The five key elements of the swing

All human movement that needs skilful repetition contains five important elements which need to be effectively balanced to get the best out of that particular movement. The golf swing, no less than any other kinetic skill, requires its fair share of these basic factors. They are *space, time, weight, force* and *flow*. They are interrelated, but they can be described and checked separately in their role in the golf swing, as I will show below. They are, by the way, excellent for improving the kinesthetics of a player because among their many facets, they increase the depth of feeling, or awareness.

Left: *The force he's gathered in the way of 'energy collection' on the backswing will be transposed into the flow of the forward swing. There will be no need to apply extra force to the shot: enough is already contained in the responsive movements of the forward swing to those of his backswing. These responses alone will produce the force required.*

Right: *His superb centering and balance throughout the smooth, rhythmic swing suggest that he plays just within his own natural tolerances.*

A professional will be totally aware of these elements either by feel or absolute knowledge of them.

1. Space

The spatial factor, or the awareness of the movement in space around you, really starts in the address. You assemble yourself so that you have enough space or room to swing.

You're running out of space when your chin has sunk into your chest, your forearms are touching your sides and your feet are too close together, to say nothing of overbent knees; and, at the other extreme, when your hands are too near the ground, pulling your spinal angle into a slump. An overdose of muscular relaxation and you are quickly running out of working space.

In the dynamic part of the swing the awareness of making a good-size wheel in the space around you is particularly important. The size of the half-wheel on the backswing tends to determine a similar and more balanced half for the rest of the swing unit.

If you bite off more space than you can chew, it will pull you out of centre and ruin your chances of making a good shot. On the other hand, if you're too mean with your space you'll find it well nigh impossible to generate a reasonable clubhead speed.

I've always been impressed with the amount of space Gary Player uses at his assembly. He occupies quite a generous amount of space here and it's not difficult to imagine that he's set fair for making a large, powerful arc. His rather longer than average golf clubs however do steal a spot more space and thereby bring him nearer to the space-eating swing size of some of his taller and broader colleagues and rivals.

Flat planes, medium planes or upright planes do not differ in the amount of space they utilize; they are just taking up space at slightly different angles.

The body coils and uncoils in its *own* space in a golf swing. In other words it does not use up 'swing' space. Even its final spiral is (ideally) kept on centre, but there is a certain amount of acceptable tolerance within the limits of balance after the ball has gone. There is nothing more undignified than falling on your backside at the end of the swing, and nothing more inhibiting than being afraid of doing so! The Puerto Rican-born US star Chi-Chi Rodriguez has been known to swing so fast and to use up so much speed at the expense of balance that he has finished sitting down at the end of some of his prodigiously long shots. He certainly uses a lot of 'space' for a little fellow.

2. Time

This means exactly what it says. The professionals will be just as aware of the time they take to perform their pre-shot drill as they will be of the time they take to actually play the shot. They will, over a period, develop a fixed time for this preparation. Bobby Locke was the finest example of a fixed pre-shot routine and he took exactly the same time every time before he moved into action.

The story of James Braid's preparations before a shot is legendary. Braid was one of the great triumvirate of the Vardon-Braid-Taylor era before the First World War. Later, when he was professional to Walton Heath, he was once playing with a member of that prestigious club who got a little tetchy over Braid's 'waggles'. At one hole the members said to Braid, 'You've already had *twelve* waggles'. During the 13th, Braid stopped and said in reply, 'You're quite right, sir. And now,' – there was a slight pause – 'I'm going to start all over again!'

The time taken over assembly is not critical as long as it is not hurried or subject to freezing. A good professional player will stick to his timed preparation regardless of the pressures he is under. The poor handicap player will get a shot over as quickly as possible in a futile attempt to evade any pressure, however small. But this only adds fuel to the fire, of course.

It's a good exercise to actually time yourself on your preparation and try to repeat it on every shot you play. Time consuming? Not really. After all, if you then hit better shots so much time is saved that would otherwise be taken up looking for the ball in the rough or the woods! Good shots make for a lighter heart and quicker steps; bad shots are the precursors of a heavy heart and slower steps.

I played behind Henry Cotton once in a tournament. My partner and I waited on practically every shot. 'The maestro won't be playing well today,' said my partner, 'but he'll score well'. I was later to play with Cotton in the qualifying rounds of his last Open. He played well and so did I – and found him the most pleasant and encouraging partner I'd ever had in a tournament.

A number of my pupils have said to me that they have found difficulty in starting the backswing. When this happens it usually heralds the onset of a hurried and shortened version. Once again, they are glad 'to get it over with.' The remedy is quite simple – and always works. Take a little of that time allotted for the swing in pushing forwards a fraction *before* starting back. This forward press can be with the hands or the knees or both. And I mean forwards in the direction of the target, so that there will be no suggestion of a swing diversion. I make no apologies for repeating the value of the forward press (see chapter 4) or what could be described as a 'kick-start': it certainly helps to trigger off that time factor.

A quick, snatchy start back isn't the pace of the professionals. There's normally a lot of deliberation on the backswing. It was best described by Irv Schloss as 'leisurely'. The speed increases as the swing progresses, he used to say. 'The fastest segment is your impact-to-swing finish'.

'Progressive acceleration' might well describe the overall type of speed best suited to a golf swing, but the handicap golfer is more likely to rush the backswing and slow down or decelerate on the forward swing. Unfortunately every golfer does not possess the right temperament to do this naturally or without deliberation and thought. The natural 'slasher' will pay little heed to rhythm, while the opposite personality, the lethargic type, doesn't generate enough clubhead speed to hit the ball very far even if it does do a 'Bing Crosby' and 'go straight down the middle'.

Effective speed, tempo or rhythm needs a lot of disciplined practice.

3. Weight

Awareness of weight at assembly is quite measurable in the way it's dispensed between the feet. So is the transference (or non-transference) of weight on the backswing – and there should be none worth noticing. On the forward swing the transference of whatever weight there was on the right foot should be shed noticeably to the left foot with the minimum remaining to help the right foot support the balance.

There's a popular fallacy that weight and pressure are the same thing. They are not. While the weight of the body is a constant tangible condition, pressure is variable, the result of applied force. When you squeeze the insides of your knees in a little and grip a little more firmly on the insides of your shoes at assembly, you're exerting pressure over a specific area. When you press a little more firmly with those last three left-hand fingers you're exerting pressure.

The pressure of a pinpoint on a table can exert more force over its area than the weight of an elephant's foot over its own area. This is precisely why golf shoes won't damage a golf green even when worn by a giant, while a petite lady wearing stiletto heels can do an awful lot of damage. It's why broad-rimmed golf trolleys are acceptable on a golf course but narrow-wheeled trolleys are not. The pull of gravity transmits the feel of weight in a movement, so the weight distribution must be specially arranged to offset the force of gravity on steep slopes. The steeper these are, the more the weight positioning is affected.

The feel of the weight displacement is lighter at speed, but it's more easily shifted off centre. By expert centre control, the pros overcome for the most part the very common fault of the handicap player, swaying, which is basically caused by a poor sense of what's happening to the body weight during a swing.

4. Force and 5. Flow

These are the outcome of the combined sequence of movements emanating from the static assembly, the size of the swing's arc, the coil of the body against the base as a result of this and the responsive change of direction of the arms unit, and the action and reaction of this on the body and legs.

The arms swing unit does not in itself supply all the swing force or flow. It derives quite a lot of energy from the body's response to this swing. The arms swing in the first place feeds the body and the body responds by feeding the arms with even more energy.

Force isn't something that explodes just into the back of the ball, taking it by surprise. It's a gradual accumulation of positive energy which takes the ball in its stride as it increases in its crescendo of spontaneous acceleration until the energy is spent.

Force is a co-ordinated flow of 'return swing deviations'.

CHAPTER TEN

GOLF AND THE LAWS OF PHYSICS

The laws of physics can be applied to all the components of the golf swing; indeed, as we shall see, they actually govern them to a large extent. These not only help reveal the common factors of most playing methods but also prove the importance of those factors in making the swing viable. In other words, you can't do it without them. Yet so many amateurs of all levels waste valuable time and energy in a running battle with these laws, constantly trying to defy them, mainly because they don't understand a few elementary principles of movement.

Uniform circular motion

'Natural' unimpaired acceleration from the change of direction at the top of the backswing keeps the radius (club) at right-angles to the arc of the swing and maintains the correct speed. If the speed of the swing is altered the shot will be spoilt. Any attempt after starting the downswing to enhance this natural acceleration by hitting harder or 'flicking' will decelerate the swing and almost certainly divert its path. As Ben Hogan so succinctly put it: 'Once you've changed direction it's too late to change your mind.'

The conical pendulum

In the golf swing the body revolves with uniform circular motion in a horizontal circle about the vertical axis. There are two forces involved, acting in opposite directions: one is the weight of the clubhead bearing vertically downwards (mg), and the other is the tension along the shaft and arms (t). The combined result is centripetal force (see diagram), directed toward the centre of the arc (*o*). For different speeds of swings the angle of body and arms (*a*) must be changed to satisfy this condition, and as different clubs have differing speeds in the swing, it follows that the angle between the body and arms must also change with the choice of club.

Centripetal force

This is essentially a component of gravity, an upward and inward force from the inside of the feet up to the hips. It operates in both the static and dynamic phases, and quite simply helps to secure your grip on the ground. This explains why it's necessary to make allowances in the assembly for slopes.

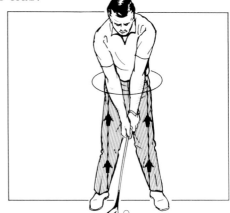

On an up-slope, the pressure at assembly should be directed more towards the left foot and against the hill; on a down-slope the pressure should be against the hill and towards the right foot.

Many professionals lift the left heel on the backswing, a characteristic often dictated by the physique of the player. Generally, the more rotund the player the more it may be necessary for him to raise the heel to allow the body to coil. But there's a limit to this, and that limit is determined by the need to retain the benefit of centripetal force. Otherwise the swing would fly vertically or laterally off centre.

Centrifugal force

This is the equal and opposite force to centripetal force, acting downwards and outwards through contact. The force bends the shaft out to the ball, while the inertia in the ball bends it back to 'right'. It's generally held by pros that slightly sunken wrists at assembly will help counteract the effect of centrifugal force, since on contact

the hands and wrists are forced into an arch which bows out the shaft, forcing the toe of the club down and the heel of the club up to the player.

Compensation for this could be holding the heel to the ball at assembly rather than the centre. Fuzzy Zoeller places the clubhead outside the ball and in my opinion allows correctly for the effects of centrifugal force on the shaft. It does induce the 'inside' swing path, of course, and the best line for the forward swing to take for optimum contact – a path which Zoeller takes with mechanical regularity and precision.

Holding the toe of the club nearer to you can only lead to returning the swing path outside that of the backswing, with all the attendant dangers – 'socketing' being the most insidious.

Angular acceleration

On the backswing the coiling of the body from the shoulders to the hips helps the arms and hands to collect potential energy. The uncoiling action of the forward swing transmits kinetic energy. The nearer the power is to the centre of acceleration the more efficiently it can pass it on to the extremities (the hands). In golfing terms, when the hands are further away from the hips, the use of the hands to develop clubhead speed will be less effective than the use of the trunk and thighs to do the same job.

I believe it was Ken Venturi, a fine American player and coach, who said that all the longest hitters had their hands nearer to their knees on the forward swing through the contact area, thus bringing the weight nearer to the axis. It's simply a case of efficient transmission of power: the further away the hands, the more distance the energy has to travel, with a resultant loss of power.

The effects of centrifugal force arching the hands through contact

must increase the gap between the hands and knees. The Venturi idea is to minimize this and return the swing on an 'inside' path, thus conforming to the principles of angular acceleration.

Inertia

When applied to the golf swing, mechanics aren't confined to those laws of physics concerned with circular motion; there are many other aspects to be considered. When the clubhead is at rest behind the ball, for example, immediately before being pulled away, it is reluctant to move. Like the golf ball, it would be content to stay there forever. It's only the force you exert on it by moving the shaft to which the clubhead is attached which makes it move at all.

The property it possesses is called inertia. This may sound trite, but it's so strong that the steel shaft actually has to bend before it's overcome and the clubhead begins to move.

Once mobile, the clubhead which was so reluctant to move at all is now equally reluctant to stop. Yet it must do this at the top of the backswing before it can change direction. This phenomenon goes a long way to explaining why so many inexperienced players tend to 'collapse' up there. Many of the more delicately muscled ladies also experience great difficulty in holding the clubhead in check at the top of the golf swing.

Having reached the top of the backswing, the clubhead has again come to rest and literally needs pulling into motion once more. The 'strong hands' brigade can achieve this more easily than the weaker fraternity or sorority, who need to exert a more conscious pull; yet it's amazing how a slight knee shuffle to the left assists the directional change of the arms and overcomes the inertia at this point in the swing. The John Reece story (see page 58) is a perfect example of alternative ways of overcoming clubhead inertia.

Potential and kinetic energy

The collection of *potential energy*, the energy of position or configuration, can be compared to the coiling of a spring. That energy, released when the spring uncoils, is just like the coiling and uncoiling of the body in a golf swing. When the arms extend backwards these too are gathering potential energy. The larger the arc of the swing, the more energy will be collected.

Torque is the energy generated by the coiling of the body and this also receives some of its energy from the arms and club arc. Torque needs resistance to help keep the swing centred; without this you would probably reach the top of the backswing facing backwards! This should not be confused with *torsion*, which is the degree of tension in a twisting or coiling action.

The right leg holding in towards the left throughout the backswing is the main source of resistance to torque. However, holding the centre with the head, and maintaining the base on that centre, from the knees down to the feet, completes the mechanisms for resisting torque in the backswing.

The energy possessed by an object by virtue of its motion (the release of potential energy) is called *kinetic energy*. Thus as kinetic energy increases, so potential energy decreases.

The forward swing contains kinetic energy, the energy of motion. The continuity of this motion also dependent on the mass and the velocity of the whole swing movement, or *momentum*. If enough potential energy has not been collected on the backswing, more kinetic energy cannot be gained by trying to apply it on the forward swing.

The professionals' adherence to centering is an outstanding feature of their swings. The club golfer tends to sway about like corn in a gale and this is the cause of many of their swing faults. Conversely, a rigid and unyielding centre inhibits extension and coil. The forces released in a golf swing must conform to the laws of motion and have an equal and opposite reaction to every action that takes place.

'Human' interference

Of course, the human mind can also 'interfere' with these mechanics as it reels off a number of negative thoughts: 'I hope it doesn't go into those trees or that lake'; or 'Oh dear, here comes Jones – I never can hit a decent shot when he's around'; or 'I must get off this tee before the three-ball comes off the green!'

A human being, unlike a piece of wood or metal, can unconsciously try to defy mechanics, particularly when the mind promotes pressure, whether real or imaginary. A classic example of this was during a Pro-Celebrity Tournament relayed on television, with Gary Player and Arnold Palmer the professionals. At one hole, Player had hit the fairway five times, but on the sixth occasion he missed it. He said to Palmer, 'I was wondering if I was going to hit this fairway for six consecutive times. That was the mistake. I wonder just why we should make such a thought?' 'It's hard to say', replied Palmer, 'but we always seem to do it.' This little episode demonstrates how the human brain can 'interfere' with mechanics, whereas machinery automatically conforms to those laws.

The tools of the trade

Whenever I visited Irv Schloss in Florida I spent a lot of time watching him make golf clubs, and on occasion helping him. He had a workshop overflowing with fascinating machines for making clubs, most of which he designed himself.

There was a machine for measuring, setting or resetting the loft and lie of iron clubs, and another for cutting out the space for a face inset in a wooden club. This looked like a huge, red, metal crab, and at the touch of a switch it clawed out the wood with a transversely moving arm. Another was set up to measure the length of shafts and, with a few rapid turns of a viciously sharp wheel, it cut the shaft the intended length. There was an air compressor which huffed and puffed as it blew grips off, and sucked and groaned as it drew them on.

The drill press, designed to drill the necks of wood heads in eight different directions, looked like a launching pad for a miniature space rocket. Numerous drill presses stood sentinel over finishers, lathes, vices and an electric device for whipping or binding the necks of wooden clubs. There was such a myriad of minor tools that you would be hard pressed to pick out a hammer easily. There were shafts, grips, iron heads, wooden heads and golf clubs in an embryonic state decorating the benches and, as you looked along, completed sets of irons and wood began to sprout from the engaging chaos, gleamingly polished from tins of dripping varnish and spinning buffers, each ready for and as individual as its customer.

I shall never forget Irv, plump and white-haired, wearing a rimless white trilby to keep the dust from his prolific locks and 'be-aproned', pouring over the swing weight machine, or drilling a wood neck, dipping a head, busily tripping along the aisle of cluttered benches or, bespectacled, checking the specification sheet of a current consignment.

Nothing would satisfy me until I had a workshop full of equipment like this. I bought a lot of machines from Irv and absorbed his ideas for making my own, or at least I had someone make them for me. That was Glyn Rowland, my head assistant at Abridge, who I sent to Florida to learn from the maestro. Well, I think he took some unique ideas with him, including a foot-pedalled air compressor, much to the delight of Irv and of Frank Harris, who partnered Irv for a while. Glyn returned to Abridge a clubmaker in everything but experience, which the intervening seven years have now made good.

Variation in clubs

A good golfer can often justifiably blame his tools. When you can't use one particular club in your set it is more than likely that it is out of balance with all the others: a different loft, lie, length, weight or grip thickness. It usually shows on a wood in worn varnish at one spot more than another. Glyn is an expert on club fault analysis.

We weigh all our components and label each one. It is remarkable how little tolerance there is in the grips, which vary by only three grams, but how much variation there is in the shafts – plus or minus six grams – while the heads vary by as much as nine grams per similar unit. Taking measurements makes it much easier to select components to make a truly matched set.

At the moment Glyn is making a device for measuring shaft frequencies or oscillations to the needs of the customer, but it is our private view that there will be little if any difference in selection from that which we already get with our extremely accurate weight measured components. Swing weighting, too, is a much more simple task with component selection. There is no need, as a lot of manufacturers do, to ram the swing weighting down the hosel.

The Schloss philosophy on golf clubs can be summarized as follows. Commercially manufactured clubs are mass produced. The emphasis is on cosmetics. They have two prices – wholesale and retail. They are normally all made to a standard specification but can be altered for a price and for delivery at some, often considerable, time.

Custom-made clubs are made by craftsmen for a surprisingly lower price than the assembly line manufacturer and delivery is rarely more than two weeks, sometimes less than one week. The craftsman has more time for component selection than in a large manufacturing plant, of course.

Components and materials

Shafts are the heart of all golf clubs. They usually come in five different flexes, but the assembly line clubmakers pay little if any regard to tolerances. The craftsman checks and matches shafts.

During play the grip is the only contact you have with your golf club, so it's very important to have the grip sized to fit your hands. Most grips are of man-made materials and vary in size from the smallest female hand to the largest hand. Leather grips are still available and there are even special grips for those with arthritis.

Heads of golf clubs vary in style more than form, and while the faces and necks of irons have been 'refined', they have undergone little essential change since the advent of steel shafts. One would be struggling to defend anything but a solid back on these irons, especially behind the hitting surface. Although variations in these backs will come and go, the differences are largely cosmetic rather than technical.

Woods are available in limitless variations, but they have not basically changed since the set of 'Bobby Jones' introduced by A. G. Spalding Bros in the early 1930s.

Most wood heads are made of laminated maple, persimmon (American date-palm) or other woods. Though persimmon heads are considered by many as premium, laminated heads may be better for you because of their durability. There is no proven difference in feel or distance in persimmon or laminated.

Face materials have been added to woods to improve durability, and high-numbered woods such as the 5, 6, 7, 8 or even more are now available. Metal 'woods' have not changed much in form.

Modern irons are made in two different ways – investment cast stainless

THE SIGNIFICANCE OF BALL SIZE

Allow me to make a brief historical resume before looking at the role of the ball on modern play techniques. Before 1848 the 'feathery' held sway – a leather panelled stitched case stuffed with 2.7 pennyweights. Then the 'gutty' was introduced, and the feathery was condemned forever to the museums. This was a solid piece of gutta percha rubber, but at the turn of century it suffered the same fate as the feathery when the Haskell, a rubber cored ball with a balata cover, came into use. This flew higher and further than the gutty and as there were no restrictions on size or weight, golfers enjoyed a beanfeast of longer hitting.

In 1912 Dunlop made a very small ball which added to this 'down the fairway' bonanza, and golf clubs were having to look for more land to increase the size of their courses in efforts to contain it. By 1921 the Royal and Ancient, the ruling body of golf in the British Isles, made regulations to limit the size of the golf ball in this country to 1.62 inches and the weight to 1.62 ounces. There was no such regulation until 1929 in the United States where, no doubt because of the vast amount of land at their disposal, lengthening courses and making new ones longer was no problem.

During the last few years of the 19th century and in the opening years of the 20th, British professionals had pioneered their methods in America, based on a larger sized ball. When the Americans came over to Britain to play international matches in the early 1920s, they were astonished to find a totally different swing method from that which they had been taught by Vardon and his contemporaries. It was a method based on getting the small ball away, wristy and fraught with the risks that go with an uneconomical movement. Such a method would engender brilliance staked with uncertainty. It was instinctive more than scientific.

The American method, based on a larger ball which needed driving away rather than flicking away, was founded on economy and physics, and this produced a more mechanical or robot-like movement. It was not really surprising that the Americans gained such supremacy in the golfing world as they did between the wars and to the present day.

It was easy to switch from a large ball to a small ball using the large ball method. But it wasn't so simple in reverse, as when both amateur and professional British teams had to travel to the United States to play American teams.

Very few visiting British professionals, if any, were successful in

Can a workman blame his tools? This student has come into the contact area with hardly a blemish on his swing, but just look at that shaft and clubhead – the distortion is quite pronounced. He probably made contact on the toe of the club, and may need a stiffer shaft. So much torsion, or twist, is unusual in a steel-shafted club.

American tournaments from the 1920s to the 1950s. But the Americans making the trip to Britain were able to snatch the lion's share of the events in which they participated.

Attempts were made in the 1950s to introduce an internationally uniform size ball, but they came to nothing. In the 1960s the 'R & A' made it compulsory to play the larger American ball in the Open Championship. Before this, the PGA had made the 1.68in ball compulsory for all the professional tournaments. It was obviously going to take some time before the effects of playing the big ball had conveyed its ultimate benefits to the British and European players. When it did, the American dominance subsided as the players on this side of the Atlantic took advantage of their new-found equality.

I remember chatting to David Graham, the highly skilful and successful Australian player who went to the States to compete in the 1970s. He took with him the 'small-ball wristy swing' and realized that he couldn't hope to be successful with it. He just had to change. 'It took me over four years,' he explained, 'to make the adjustments.'

Obviously, my own 'forward drive' method is based on using the larger ball. I still call it an 'American' method as opposed to a 'British' method, but the ball has influenced it far more than nationality.

My head assistant Glyn Rowland carefully selects club components for their uniformity to match up a set. The good custom clubmaker is both patient and conscientious.

steel and forged iron heads are either stainless or chrome plated. Both metal 'wood' heads and stainless steel 'iron' heads are investment cast using the 'lost wax process', which makes each casting an exact duplicate of the original.

Forged iron heads are ground into final shape, scored, polished and then chrome plated. Some people believe that the forged irons feel 'softer' than stainless, but this is a myth. In test after test where painted heads of the two materials were used, professional golfers could tell no difference.

Professional players can pick up almost any club and produce good shots, but in most cases the professional player obviously has his custom-made. The leading pros are paid to represent a golf club company and that company's name appears on their equipment. This does not mean that they would necessarily choose this equipment if money was not an influence!

A perfect technique and clubs to match make a lot of sense.

CHAPTER ELEVEN

BEATING THE SHORT GAME

If you analyse the professionals' short game techniques you'll find all the common factors of the long game, but on a reduced scale. It's also noticeable that they all play these shots with a specific rhythm, tempo or timing, just as they do with the long shots, but at a considerably slower speed.

It's an exaggeration to say that you could just take the normal start of the backswing of a drive to describe the start-back of a 50-yard approach shot. You couldn't. The 'influence' of a driver is too vastly different from that of a pitching wedge, or a sand-iron, right down to a short-held 6-iron, all of which are used for providing different types of approach shots, from a high pitching ball to a low running shot.

The professional player can, and often does, play low shots with a wedge or a sand-iron as well as with the 'choked down' other irons to keep the ball down. The value of a low flying wedge shot, either a pitching or sand-wedge, is the high amount of spin which it imparts together with the lower flight, as opposed to the lesser amount of spin on the longer clubs which can be used for short approach shots.

It's essential for any ambitious golfer to learn how to play low shots with the wedges. The simplest way is to include in the practice session about 20 shots with a wedge. At first the distance need only be short, but this should be increased by steps of five yards or so up to 50 yards.

Placement of the ball

The obvious technique you will latch on to is to play the shots with the ball placed back towards your right foot, with your hands more ahead of the ball. The danger here is that you will let your swing centre drop to the right to bring the ball back into centre; the trick is that while changing the normal ball position you retain the normal centre. You may also react by letting your hands curve your wrists to the right. This is flexion, or 'abduction'. It certainly won't feel good at first to have your hands leading the clubhead as much as the new ball position needs, but you'll get used to it.

The weight of the wedges is so much heavier than that of the woods and longer irons, despite being shorter – and they are made even shorter by the need to hold them well down the grip to shorten the radius so necessary to help to cut down the length of the shot. What's more, a shortened hold will

READY FOR THE ROUGH

Every player, no matter how good, finds himself veering off the fairway and into the rough at some time. But while the pros can take it all in their stride, the poorer amateur can fall victim to instant panic. You may well be able to recover, of course, but the golden rule is to play safe. If you're in trouble then an ambitious recovery shot – from a difficult lie and round some trees, for example – may cost you very dear if you fail. We all like to think of ourselves as some weekend Ballesteros or Norman in this respect, working miracles from impossible positions, but all too often our lack of star quality brings us down to earth with a bump. A short shot to the safety of the fairway is frequently a better bet than a spectacular attempt to beat the odds.

It may be your good fortune to find your ball sitting up so well that it couldn't have been better on the fairway. Your only problem then is the choice of club to reach (or get as near to) your target without going over an inordinate amount of more rough or other hazards to get there, if that can be avoided.

There are so many permutations of lie, position, terrain and so on that we can't deal with every situation here. But it's worth making a few general points:

1. Watch your ball carefully; it's amazing how easily a ball can disappear, even in light rough.
2. The more buried the lie, the less ambitious you should be. There is no margin of error to play with, so play safe and simply get out of trouble.
3. If you are in any doubt about what to do then, again, play safe. You'll have a better chance of making your next, 'conventional' shot pay off and regain par than the one from the rough.

pull the spine down to an angle nearly parallel to the ground, which brings the head almost directly above the ball. This combination contributes to a very upright swing plane indeed.

The weight and the continuity of the swing reacts quickly on the wrists, which therefore break almost immediately the swing begins. A short swing will cause less wrist reaction than a longer one, but it will increase as the swing lengthens for longer shots.

There isn't the need for coil in the short shot, nor should there be such leverage. The legs respond very little indeed, if at all, on the backswing.

4. Thick, heavy rough can be split with a sharp-edged wedge or a 9-iron. Long wet grass, too, is more easily demolished with a keen edge rather than one with a thick flange.
5. Heather can be a real problem, and should be treated with great respect. As a broad rule, take the shortest route to the fairway.
6. Practise your drives and long irons so that you go into the rough less often!

Swinging in the rough

The amateur will often try to 'scoop' the ball out and tend to fall back to the right in the process. But there's little chance of getting through the ball and the long grass that way.

The professional will swing through the ball, the grass and, within reason, anything else. He will move his body forwards, especially his 'undercarriage', to generate power in the swing. He won't try to 'scoop'; it will be a strong down-and-through flow of arms, club and legs past a well-held centre.

The pros try to keep as close as possible to their normal swing movement, though if the growth is tough they may exert more finger pressure to insure against grip twist.

In order to strike a ball before the foliage – or at least to contact as little of the intervening foliage before the ball – they will stand with the ball central or even right of centre between their feet. This 'narrows' the arc of the backswing and the descending approach to the ball is more likely to contact it first. A more 'wristy' backswing than normal can also help here.

Strangely enough the rules of golf do not mention the 'rough' at all. It is not a hazard as such, and is merely included in the definition of 'through the green'.

And while the arms are anything but soft or loose, there is no need for lateral width and no weight transference.

The wrist angle collection is retained on the forward swing so that in effect the hands stay ahead of the clubhead through contact. But you must remember that the arching effect of centrifugal force will dissipate the wrist angle and square up the face of the club.

There is no need, either, for applied or responsive counter-clock rotation, for there is so little clockwise rotation on the backswing, if any, to respond to. Who wants to turn the face of the club on a short shot, in or out, on and through contact? If, by the way, you are striking the ball with a turning clubface, the ball will fly left or right according to the way the face is turning; the flight of the ball will tell you which way. So you learn to hold the clubface square on these 'tournament winners'. Even at normal swing speed you should learn to become aware of this. There can be no excuse, nor should you excuse yourself, for not knowing this simple swing technique. The legs work a little with the forward swing in response to the pressure of the arms and club moving that way, and this does help to insure against the possible errant movement of the shoulders.

'Knowing is doing'

I don't believe that you can play good approach shots, or any other shot, if you don't know completely how and why the technique works. Knowing is doing. So, have not the slightest doubt in your mind that you're pressing the right buttons.

A knowledge of the physics of the short swing is equally as important as that of the technique. The laws of inertia, continuity and the collection of potential energy in the backswing will respond as kinetic energy in the forward swing here just as much as they do in the 'big swing'. Centrifugal and centripetal force come into play just as effectively with a wedge as with a 1-iron. Knowing *how* it works makes it so much easier to let it all work – rather than playing in the dark. Understanding is doing.

You may be able to play a piano by ear, but if you cannot read music you will never play in an orchestra. You can't expect to sidestep the issue of technique and then unreasonably presume it will suddenly all come together one day out of the blue. It won't.

Vardon, Jones, Hagen, Cotton, Nelson, Hogan, Player, Palmer, Nicklaus, Watson, Norman and the rest reached the top by toil as well as talent. Yet here we are, you and me, still looking for the secret formula - the easy way to success without work, time, patience, dedication and sacrifice! Knowing the technique, the physics and the contents of kinesthetic skills must help to make that work so much easier, in order that work and time need not be wasted. You should look for space, time, flow, energy and speed even in the short game; it's all there.

Top Kentucky pro Jim Owen demonstrates the perfect bunker shot. At assembly (top left) his knees are slightly bent, and he has an upright backswing with an early wrist angle collection (top centre), which steepens the forward swing into the sand. This is a universally accepted approach and very safe method. With the hands leading the clubhead through the rest of the swing, the ball is virtually sliced out of the bunker (remaining six photographs).

Ronan Rafferty is a perfect example of the European adaptation to the large ball. Only a few years ago it would have been difficult to find a European professional with these ingredients, especially with his hands so clearly ahead

When you've nearly perfected your technique you'll know simply by feel when something is misbehaving. Feedback is as useful to a golfer and his teacher as a stethoscope is to a doctor. That little ball will tell you nearly all you need to know about where the last swing went wrong. Correction is then so simple. As I pointed out in my *Newnes All-Colour Guide to Golf*, six out of six of the contact errors are on the clubface. Good technique is designed to give you optimum control of that critical area.

Approaching the approach shot

With most short shots where height and maximum spin are required the pros are trying to strike a descending blow. When they are looking for a low shot the path through the ball will be less than descending, almost ascending, short of topping it but more like a putt, where the clubhead is held low to the ground without it going into the ground.

You can slice the ball off the ground too like a bunker shot, swinging

of the clubhead through contact. But for the short-pitch shots it's a must.
There's no need for counter-clockwise rotation. Note his abducted left wrist
(see page 65) and his knees flexing just a little to target.

along a line which is parallel to the feet but leftward across the target line, with the clubface held square or even slightly open to your target throughout the stroke. The clubhead must never be allowed to be overtaken by the hands and, as in bunker shots, you must stay centered.

Another shot, another piece of music to be learned. This is played with the hands acting as a unit. The left arm tends to predominate as an unbroken radius, the right supports and the knees and legs respond. The body must stay well centered and the directional change should always be unhurried.

The creative approach

While I was in Sweden last summer it was my privilege to play on the beautiful but tough seaside links of the Ljunghusen Golf Club at Hollviksnas, near Malmö, on the shores of the Baltic Sea. With the water hazards, natural sand bunkers and heather fiendishly and jealously

*My short spin shot with a wedge; it could be described as a bunker shot
without the slice across it and striking the ball before the ground. Nor is it so
wristy on the backswing.*

guarding every green and fairway, not to mention a strongish breeze
teasing every shot hit slightly off line into deep trouble, it presents a severe
test both of skill and nerve.

I had a particularly difficult patch trying to stop the ball near the pin
from 50 yards and less off the green. In fact it was not so much a problem of
stopping the ball near the pin but actually keeping it on the green. It was
impossible to get pitch-and-putt birdies on the par-fives but also to save
pars on the long par-fours after missing greens with the second shot.

It was with the intention of solving the problem of this errant shot, that I
decided to go to the practice ground to see if I could conjure up something
that would pitch and at least not run so far or so enthusiastically for the
rough, water or sand lying as rearguard behind those Ljunghusen greens –
greens which were in magnificent shape but as fast as lightning.

Now, I know that the 'run shot' is favoured by a lot of good players,
particularly on the seaside links. The St Andrews run shot is still a
favourite of the experts, amateur or professional, who regularly play there,
and I've no criticism whatever of it. Indeed it's highly skilful. I just wanted
to prove to myself that provided I was not pitching onto a concrete path or a
metalled road I could impart effective spin with a wedge.

I tried using my two sand-irons, one a broad sole, the other a narrow sole,
but these also failed to stop the ball within a reasonable putting distance.

As I've said, it's not uncommon for professionals to devise special shots

Notice that I've 'hinged' my left wrist but the important swing radius is completely intact. Professionals improvize such shots in practice and use them as the occasion demands in tournaments.

of their own. Irv Schloss used to say that most of the shots played below hip high could be categorized as 'specials'. Obviously I knew how to 'cut' the ball to make it spin, but this is a very wristy shot to play under pressure. I was looking for something much safer than that, something which would ensure I made centre of the clubface contact. In no way could I afford the luxury of counter-clock rotation. The face of the wedge must be kept absolutely square to target but set back, so that it was almost 'shovelling' the ball into the air but smartly, with speed, to create maximum spin.

I tried to keep a very firm left-hand grip, a firm left wrist and left elbow joint. This would at least give me support in holding the clubface in its 'to target' position. With my left arm well occupied it was now the task of my right arm and hand to deliver the blow. The best way I can describe this would be like shaking a frying pan with a pancake in it to prevent it from sticking. The shaking was in the direction of the target.

It had to be quite a hard shake to impart height into the shot and gain the required spin. It could, however, be only as hard as the length of the shot demanded – maybe from 8 to 4 on my clock system for 50 yards, even 9 to 3, and shorter for shorter shots. After a number of attempts, the ball began to react as I wanted. The swing felt rather sharp, anything but smooth, although I kept the backswing down to quite a slow speed, but the extra spin was there.

There didn't seem to be much spin at all during the flight. I could almost see the red band of the range balls looking quite static in some shots, but when they landed they were a lot less lively. They 'sat down' beautifully. Eureka! What was pleasing was that the grass marks were appearing bang in the middle of the clubface. I had double-checked that my centre was absolutely intact after a few failures. Simply enough, this was just keeping a well-centred head over the ball position throughout the stroke.

Now, how did it look? I asked Ron Duncan, a retired architect and expert cameraman, who with his wife Barbara was staying with us in Sweden, to take a 35mm motordrive sequence for me. I'll leave you to judge my improvized shot for yourself (see previous pages) . . .

Putting without panic

Putting is supposed to be the great worry or weakness of the great players. I don't believe this; they – that is the media, mainly – used to say that Henry Cotton was a bad putter. But I've seen Cotton putting, and he was quite brilliant. Because of many back-breaking hours' practice he was able to make every putt a 'straight' one and let the contour of the ground do the rest, as do all good putters. This is half the problem in putting, and half the solution: finding a straight line to a contour near the hole which runs in towards it and 'straight hitting' the ball to that spot. If there isn't a slope adjacent to the hole, the straight line must be to the hole itself.

Strength is the other half of the problem in putting. The pros practise specific putting lengths and so find the related swing lengths. Irv Schloss was one of the best putters I've every seen, even his 30-yarders could never be discounted. He swung his putter simply, with firm wrists low through, but never very far through; he used the most economical swing possible.

Putting is the one area of golf where individualistic styles are permitted and even encouraged – as long as they are justified by results – as these three members of my Abridge club illustate:

Top row: 'The Toski Trot': club captain Harvey Rose, a 6-handicap player and an excellent putter, has taken the advice of top American coach Bob Toski to 'run through the ball and not away from it' quite literally, moving after it before he's completed his follow through.

Middle row: 'The St Andrews Ladies': Barbara Klein successfully emulates some of the experts of the St Andrews Ladies' Putting Club by separating her grip – or more accurately playing with her right hand and 'guiding' the pendulum of the putter with her left hand from the top. This is an acceptable example of 'hingeing'.

Bottom row: 'The Leo Diegel System': Lady club captain Doreen Lazarus adopts the cradled elbow stance of Leo Diegel.

*Jim Owen again, this time using his two-line putting exercise. Note that his
eyes are directly above the ball, his toes are in line and his upper arms
grooved into his body. On the follow through the putter head is kept near to
the ground, with the hands moving parallel to the green. When a key action
like this becomes a habit with practice, it needn't occupy your thoughts,
leaving you free to enhance your skill.*

He looked on putting more as a geometrical problem and was great on the
theme that 'all putts are straight putts'.

It's a bit like driving your car. The more you've practised, the more
confident you will be. Equate the length of shot with the length of the
swing. It saves relying on judgment. So, practise specific lengths and you'll
begin to recognize the length of the swing required for them. The forward
swing needs nothing more than allowing the reaction of the backswing to
take over. It will respond in every way to that, if you can resist helping it.
It's an amazing sensation to feel your arms working from their own
swinging weight.

Keep a cool head. Don't press the panic button. Make your corrections at
normal speed, for any slower means more error. You can only do your best.

One final point about life on the green is worth making: that is, once that
ball has left the clubface your control over it has gone completely. I've seen
household names calling to the moving ball and demanding it to 'sit' as
though it had the receptive power of a spherical canine. These could only
be like echoes which bounce back to the caller – or cunning professionals
playing to the gallery, knowing the ball would curve back to target,
knowing it would eventually 'sit' in the bottom of the cup. And of course
the gallery loved it.

CHAPTER TWELVE

THE LADIES:
STUDENTS OR TEACHERS ?

'Wouldn't I be better off going to a woman teacher?' This question is frequently put to me by prospective lady students of all ages, and my reply is now virtually automatic: 'Madam, if you *feel* you'll get better results by going to a female coach, then it would be advisable to do so'. It's so vital that from the very start you have complete confidence in your teacher.

There's a growing number of women professionals who enjoy the reputation of being excellent teachers. I know two Americans, Nancy Wilbert of Florida and Monica Darling of Massachusetts, who opted for coaching instead of playing the pro tour, and with great success. Nancy, incidentally, is also an expert clubmaker and repairer.

In my view there's no conceivable reason why a woman teacher shouldn't be just as effective as a man – or any better. But it's not because she may know more about the anatomy, physiology or psychology of another woman in relation to the golf swing and the golf game; it would be simply because she knows about the golf swing, the game of golf and the psychology of human reaction. Whether the humans concerned are male or female makes not the slightest difference.

The technique and psychology I've expounded in these pages is universal. The differences between the sexes, physical or psychological, just don't come into it. There's only one golf swing and only one type of psychological reaction to success or failure for all players, male or female. No awkward or embarrassing questions need therefore be asked by the student, so there's nothing to answer by the teacher.

Grace and favour
It has long been my opinion, however, that lady golfers are more able to adopt a graceful swing movement than men. It's such a pity that they are liable to suffer more interference outside proper coaching than the men. The interference is inevitably from male golfers – husbands, boyfriends, brothers, uncles, sons, and any other amateur male coach who can't resist flaunting his knowledge on any and every unfortunate female who is industriously practising.

I shall celebrate with an extra glass of mineral water – I'm a teetotaller – the day I see a female amateur golfer teaching her husband or any other male, relative or otherwise, who was quietly rehearsing the formula he had so recently acquired from the local pro. It just doesn't happen.

There was, and probably still is, a school of thought among teaching pros that men are able to make a better backswing hip coil than ladies, although members of the medical profession say there's no reason whatsoever why this should be so. I must confess to having noticed only a very small

---

Kim Hurley (opposite), one of my students. We've modified that over-supple backswing summit and the wrist angle retention, and she comes into the contact like a champion. Both her extension and her long flowing finish exude all the airs of a top professional.

A strong girl with a determined character, South African Sonja Van Wyk (below) has an excellent swing – exuberant, forceful and very professional.

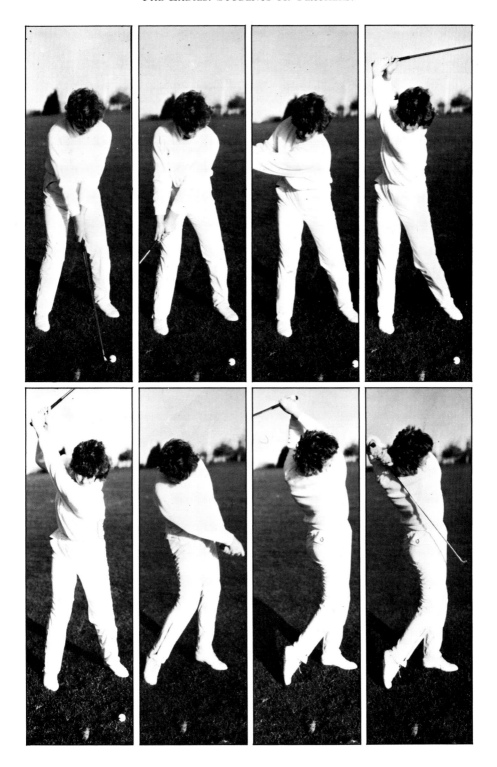

percentage of lady golfers who have some trouble with the hip coil (on the backswing), but I have noticed a similar quantity of men players who are also 'wooden' in that area.

It's true I think that generally speaking women are not quite so physically strong as men and as a result they cannot hit the golf ball the distances that men do. But then there are quite a number of women professionals and good amateurs who hit the ball well past most amateur men players.

Laura Davies hits the ball around the 300-yard mark, but like the majority of big hitters not with the consummate ease with which one would like to describe it. Rather it comes from a terrific generation of arm speed on the forward swing past a very well centered head and retained spinal angle with an excellent tempo.

The sequence of photos of my professional student Kim Hurley on page 115 shows the typical common factors of the professional swing. Though Kim isn't hefty she is capable of hitting a 7-iron shot more than 180 yards under normal conditions, and the rest of her clubs relate in length. That's no mean hitting for a slip of a lass. Like her contemporary Laura Davies, she's capable of a high-level forward swing acceleration which looks disarmingly smooth because of her superb rhythm.

Women club golfers do not, and in many cases cannot, reach the acceleration enjoyed by the professionals. Many of them are really flat out without appearing to be so and are completely destroyed when urged to 'speed up' by impatient and misguided husbands. Others who really can let their arms and the various responses zip through will be told to slow down. It would seem that the ladies just can't win.

I can only repeat what I've said about the men when I'm writing about the ladies in the context of overall technique: some ladies are more athletic than others, just as some men are more athletic than other men.

Advent of the golfing widower?

As with the men pros, I've seen some of the ladies out on the practice ground after a disappointing round, cutting quite lone figures in the receding light as they correct shots which let them down. But I must confess I occasionally imagine some lonely husband struggling over the complication of his evening meal. The golfing widower? The new social problem of the eighties?

It's a tough life for the women professional players. Living out of a suitcase after they have found somewhere to stay and then moving on to go through the same routine in different surroundings with the same anxieties. And yet they're a happy smiling band of humans, wonderful ambassadors for their profession and their countries.

Learning from the ladies

The men members of Abridge have now fixed an annual Lady Pro-Am tournament. They enjoyed the golf and the company of these delightful ladies, who always find time during play to help their amateur partners with their game and sympathize diplomatically, with the eternal post-mortems over tea and cakes in the clubhouse. Some of the men pros could learn a lot from the ladies about the art and value of good 'PR'.

I think the lady professionals have – either by design or chance – probably unearthed some secret or secrets of the professional game, and perhaps of the game itself. With a few exceptions a lot of these young women are little more than wisps of girls, and yet they fire the ball those ridiculously long distances with their woods and hit their irons as crisply and accurately as their male colleagues.

How? Well, their swing mechanics are very often (because of good professional coaching) as sound as good mechanics can be. They make the best of their physiques by staying cannily within their individual tolerances. Their natural tendency is to do as much as is needed for efficiency, and *only* as much as is needed rather than indulging in the luxury of pure cosmetics.

In other words, and perhaps to be a little harsh on some chaps, they discard the unnecessary gestures of the masculine 'show-off'.

It's their rhythm which casts a light on the whole picture and probably reveals one secret. When you know that you are moving in a certain way, under control, and you have done it so often you just know you can go on doing it and it makes good golf shots, your psychological reactions are that much more positive. Bad shots create frustration and gloom, good shots create pleasure and confidence.

The ladies have all the ingredients so well balanced out, and maybe we should take a leaf or two from their notebooks. Most men golfers could certainly benefit from a visit to at least one LPGA tournament.

CHAPTER THIRTEEN

MASTERING THE MIND

This chapter of the book is based on a captivating lecture given by Hubie Smith, now of the Concord Resort Hotel, Concord Master Golf Club, Kiamesha Lake, New York, a man who in 1969 was Co-National Professional of the Year in the United States. Amusingly entitled 'The Ear-to-Ear Method of Maintaining Playing Ability', it was delivered at the USPGA school at West Palm Beach, Florida, in 1972, and I was proud to be present on that occasion.

It's a brilliant yet simple summary of the best mental attitudes to playing this game of ours, for both tour and club professionals. Yet in my opinion the advice, information and messages it contains hold true for amateur players too, no matter what their standard of play.

Loss of interest

The basic reason you're a golf professional today is your original interest in golf – in fact we can say *competitive* golf. When we fail to maintain our playing ability it's normally due to loss of interest. But why do we lose interest?

Here are some of the reasons: 1 – the position requires too much of our time; 2 – a loss of desire to improve; 3 – a lack of prize money to play for; 4 – pride (not scoring as we once did proves embarrassing); 5 – competition is too tough; 6 – lack of goals.

A large percentage of us to some extent owe our present position to past playing ability. So maintaining our playing ability is part of our job. Certainly we can't play in all events in our section, but we can key in on certain ones because of their prestige or purse and not isolate ourselves completely from competition. The new friendships, the reunion with friends, and the enjoyment of competition are all worth the effort in maintaining ability.

We all know that the ideal situation is to 'practise, play and practise'. When we speak in these terms we generally think of physical activity, but most of this presentation will be about mental activity or mental practice – about mental improvement, not physical improvement.

Mental attitudes

I've been told that Byron Nelson's goal while on tour was to par all the par-three holes, par all the par-fours and birdie all the par-fives. With a normal par of 72 this would give him a score of 68. He had this attitude, for example: on a par three of 250 yards, if he should knock his tee shot within three feet of the hole, miss the putt and take three, he would walk off the green satisfied that he'd made his goal and would go on to the next tee with a positive attitude – not one of disgust and anger because he had missed the short putt. I understand that he birdied 80 per cent of the par-fives he played in competitions. He had a good mental attitude.

How often we have heard that the game is 90 per cent mental, or 50 per cent mental? Frankly, in our professional status it's probably closer to 90 than 50. We say it and we hear it, but do we believe it? Do we devote *any* time to mental practice or mental playing? Most of us have the physical ability required, so it has to be the mental ability which keeps us from maintaining our playing ability. Mental practice as opposed to physical practice doesn't even require time. I think we agree it's in our mind when we push, pull or stab shots rather than in our physical ability.

Golf is a game which can start a mental flurry in a second. Attitude costs more strokes than lack of ability. We need to develop the proper positive attitude. Don't expect too much of yourself, or set your sights too high. You don't have to think you're going to win just because you pay an entry fee. Attempt to finish well and make up your mind never to 'pick it up'. If you know you *can* pick it up then you automatically are lax in technique. How many times have you won a tournament when you thought you were going to beforehand? Almost never. You must play within your limitations. There are many things which affect mental attitudes, and here are some of them:

Excuses: If we spent as much time preparing our minds to play well as we spend thinking of excuses for playing badly, imagine the shots that would be saved. As professionals we've heard every excuse ever made. We have Jack Daniels, George Dickel and Johnny Walker; too much work, too little golf and too many women; poor pairings, poor golf courses, and poor caddies; the rain, the wind and the heat; sore feet, sore hands and sore backs; bursitis, arthritis and tendonitis. We take the credit for all good shots and blame the bad ones on something else. We attempt to protect our ego by taking the sting out of our failures by blaming others.

When we make excuses we hinder learning capacity. It makes failures more easy to take but it makes it harder to learn to improve. The least desirable person on a golf course is the griper. How often have we heard the expression, 'I can't putt'? Let me tell you this: if you *believe* it, don't tell it to anyone else. Did you ever notice that you putt well with the fellows who think you can putt and putt badly with those who know you can't putt?

Years ago I had a caddie who often used to carry for me in area tournaments, during a period when I was an extremely poor putter; any time that he caddied for me after that, I always putted badly. The same holds true with playing companions. If you've expressed time after time to people that you can't putt, they tend to believe you, and when in their company you *do* putt badly. By the same token when you have a good day on the putting green with a group you will most likely have the same experience when you play with them again. So if you believe that you can't putt, don't let anyone know or it will only compound your problem. There are thousands of reasons for failure, but not a single excuse. It's only a mental crutch.

Anger: There isn't a professional golfer anywhere who has never been angry on a golf course. We've all been angry and in all probability we will continue to become angry. We must learn to control it. In order to control anger we must first give up the feeling that we are 'entitled to become upset'. If we feel we are entitled to gripe at bad luck, the elements, barking dogs in the distance, our own inability, then the battle is virtually lost. We become an emotional cripple. Griping is at first justified for major items, then for lesser distractions; finally it becomes a senseless, self-destructive habit. It's best to give up the idea that we're justified in any anger.

Use every opportunity to practise not getting upset. It takes time, but can be learned like every other phase of the game. When an incident occurs to make you angry change it into an opportunity to improve your game. Learn to channel your anger, direct the feeling into resolution for mental practice. The more times you become angry, the better your game will become. Every missed shot produces its own correction.

Motivation to improve would soon disappear if we trained ourselves not to react to anger at all. *Useless* anger should not be permitted to develop – *useful* anger can be directed towards improvement. We can't hit bad shots *every* time if we remain free of anger. Have faith in the law of averages and expect the unexpected such as bad lies, bad bounces and bad breaks. Where did we ever get the idea that just because a ball is round it's supposed to bounce straight?

Are we not physically competent in being able to hit any type of golf shot? Can we not hit high shots, hooks and slices? Can we not hit out of a buried lie or from behind a tree? Do we always have a perfect lie and a straight shot? Have a running battle with the ball. Tell yourself that as long as you can address it, you can hit it.

Build up a philosophy which fate can't overthrow. Make it take a lot of bad breaks to make you sore. Be the happiest when you have a hard shot to make. Acquire the ability to adapt to changing circumstances. It's one of the most important skills we can have.

Fear: Confidence and fear cannot exist together in the same thought. Fear makes muscles work that shouldn't be used. Fear makes us *stupid*, and we then cannot make decisions; yet golf, especially competitive golf, is a game of decisions. Tension comes from fear of failure. There's more tension in golf than any sport. Motion is the greatest antidote for tension and there is little motion in golf compared to other sports. We have to condition ourselves mentally. Most of us when we tee the ball up in a tournament are concerned about the results rather than taking one shot and one hole at a time.

Psychologists tell us that anxiety is a common cause of drowning. When a person is in the middle of a lake and realizes that he may drown he immediately thinks of the shore or the final result, rather than taking one stroke at a time. The same applies to golf. We are too concerned with the total score than the shot in hand. The best control for fear is to *over-learn*. Do whatever we fear until we become accustomed to it. We possess the ability to control nervous tension. We can live with being nervous in a controlled state.

Many of us are afraid to win! We take the lead in a tournament and immediately the thought comes to mind, 'What am I doing here?' Then we try to disappear. And no other sport exists whereby you can disappear more rapidly than in golf. Everything we do as individuals we do because we feel it's in our best interest. No-one knowingly hurts themselves. People who have suicidal impulses lose the desire to commit suicide when they realize it's not in their best interests. Fear is the most destructive mental attitude we can have.

Cockiness: As undesirable as the term is, to be cocky can hold an advantage, especially if you can conceal this attitude so that it's not apparent to others. With players of equal ability, under pressure, the one who is cocky will produce a lower score. We're all cocky to some extent. In giving a golf clinic in front of unskilled persons, how easy it is to call a shot and then produce it with no problem at all; but before a group of fellow professionals the same shot becomes a little more difficult.

Cockiness is better than fear but it has its weaknesses. To be cocky without cause is better than to be fearful without cause, but both are faulty to some degree. Try to be as cold-blooded as possible, with no self-delusions.

Confidence: This is the most talked about of the mental attitudes, and the least understood. Absolute confidence is no guarantee of success. We tend to get false impressions of confidence. A player with confidence, but unskilled, cannot beat a player who is skilled yet lacks confidence: *psychology* cannot overcome *physics*. Many of us have false confidences in wrong methods. You may have an emotional confidence about a given club in a situation, for example, when another club would be better.

I'm reminded of Cotton Hill, of Mississippi, who has putted with the pitching wedge for several years. After missing two or three short putts at the beginning of a round of golf, he switched to a pitching wedge; and when the round was concluded he had shot a course record. From this he received an emotional confidence in the club, instead of intellectual confidence based on fact. If, over the years, he had physically and mentally practised with the putter as he had with the pitching wedge, I think we'd all agree he would have to have enjoyed more consistent results with the putter than the wedge.

We develop confidence again by 'overlearning'. When we practise and become competent with short shots, our long irons become better; when we begin to make the short putts the chipping improves. You lose the fear of having to be extra competent in certain areas. Overlearning leads to success, success to confidence, confidence leads to more success. True confidence may not be permanent. Through a series of failures we tend to lose our confidence, and then we have to overlearn again.

Concentration

The definition of concentration is to limit one's conscious thoughts to as narrow a scope as possible under existing conditions. Golf is a game of decisions, and you cannot make decisions unless you concentrate. The right kind of tension produces positive concentration. Some of us are scared to think. We hurry through the shot instead, to avoid thinking. You cannot think too much before a shot, but you can during execution. Our minds are like computers: the more we run through them the better we can make the right decision.

Distractions: Why is it that some things will disturb one person but not another? Have you ever played with a fellow who had his child or dog along with him and marvelled at how he could concentrate on a shot, while you were bugged to death? We simply look for distractions. A story is told of a caddie who was up ahead of his golfer several yards, waiting to watch the flight of the ball. The golfer would waggle, look at the caddie, waggle, look at the caddie; finally he hit and topped the shot. He turned to the caddie and said, 'Why did you move?' 'I didn't move a muscle,' replied the caddie. 'Well, you were going to.' The distraction existed only in the player's mind.

Gimmicks: It always helps the concentration to have one or two gimmicks. They may change from time to time to be effective, but you should have them with you constantly.

Practice

In our profession time is of the essence, and therefore we must specialize in our practice sessions. If we could spend 15 to 30 minutes in a specialized session of physical practice on a given shot or club, the confidence we would gain in this short period may stay with us for a six-month period. But you must first practise physical weaknesses; do not practise strengths.

The average professional will usually have a gallery when he goes to the practice tee. Never do we get to practise in solitude. Therefore our practice sessions are different. With a gallery we tend to practise our strengths, to show off a little. We get more pleasure out of practising the shots we can hit than we do those that cause the trouble. We simply do not have the courage to make a public display of our weak shots. But you must practise your weaknesses if you expect an improvement in that area of your scoring.

The law of dimishing returns: It can be dangerous to try to become too good with any one club. There comes a point when additional practice will not produce an equivalent improvement in score. Practise one shot too much and an analysis of your score may well show diminishing returns.

Practice does not make perfect: Practice does not make perfect when we practise strengths – when we practise shots where there is no demand, such as using long irons when you're going to play a tournament on a course that will be all pitch and putt. Your score won't show any results from this type of practice. You must practise to hold your present ability, but to improve it requires more work.

Mental practice: Mental practice requires none of your time, only your thoughts. You should practice your psychological weaknesses just like you do the physical ones. The nervous system controls your complete physical activity–timing, physical shape and muscle tone. Never go into a tournament in which you expect to do well mentally cold. Think about the event three or four days before. You're better off to go into the tournament physically cold than mentally. Preparation breeds success.

The subconscious mind is the workshop of thought. The conscious mind does what the subconscious says. Reflex actions and quick thinking are part of the subconscious mind. Jinx shots make jinx holes and jinx holes make jinx tournaments. Do you ever stop to think what makes a jinx hole? Experimenting of course, not hitting a normal shot, trying something other than routine method. More shots are lost because of poor thinking than lack of physical ability.

Did you ever lay awake the night before a tournament thinking about the 'troublesome' 11th hole, then go out the very next day and play it just like you thought – badly. This is a thinking weakness. The brain reacts like a computer, so make sure you feed it the right information if you want the right results. What you feed into the brain comes out as a direction to the muscles. Practise positive thinking and you get positive results.

Thinking errors tend to repeat just like physical errors. Never implant in your mind a bad thought such as 'shank', missing short putts, hooking when you need a fade, and so on. Practise positive thoughts. The eighth hole at the Cookville Country Club has an out of bounds on the left. Many times have I seen golfers slice for seven consecutive holes and then hook out of bounds on the eighth. The only possible explanation is that the brain computer has been fed the message, don't hook, don't hook, don't hook, into it. What else could the muscle do except react to a hook situation? Think positive, play positive.

Procedure and strategy

I would say that 95 per cent of us warm up physically before a tournament, 5 per cent warm up mentally. Warm up days in advance, but especially on the day of the tournament. Don't hurry to practise physically. Better not to hit any balls at all than to hurry through them. Keep in mind that the physical warm up is *only* a warm up. Why show off to the gallery any good shots while on the 'warm up' tee. I remember a tournament where I topped my initial tee shot and three-putted the last green for a 69. In passing a group of caddies near the scoreboard, I heard one of them say – he had watched me tee off and finish – 'He sure must have been lucky, he can't play.' Keep your good shots a secret until they count, because they count for nothing in the warm up.

Putting well? If the answer is yes, why practise and set up a wrong mental attitude by missing two or three short ones on the practice green? I would like to see a putting green with no cups. Getting the speed and establishing the stroke is the reason for the warm up; save the one-putts for the scoreboard.

Countdown: Set up the same each time, each shot, using the same amount of time, regardless of whether the shot is worth one dollar or a thousand dollars. There will be less chance to panic if you go through the same routine in a prescribed countdown. You don't have time to fear the results; you're concentrating on the countdown procedure.

Scoring

This is what it's all about. There are two ways to score well: hit the ball well and score well, and hit the ball badly and score well. You only have to hit three or four good shots in an 18-hole round at the right places to have an excellent score. Many professionals give up too quickly. As club professionals, without the time to devote to practise, we must realize that the wheel is going to come off somewhere during the round.

What difference does it make if you bogie or double bogie the 1st or the 18th hole? In fact, I would prefer to miss the first hole if I had a choice, since at least you have the chance to get it back. Some of your best rounds can be produced by poor beginnings, because it makes you work harder. Think of the round as a complete unit and take each shot in its stride. We have to realize that we're going to miss some shots in a round and when they appear they shouldn't come unexpectedly. Play each shot individually, without thinking of the results.

It's said that Walter Hagen hit more bad shots in one season than Harry Vardon did in a lifetime – but that Hagen beat more great players. He often said, 'Three of those and one of them counts four.' He knew that and they did not have to be four good ones. Get the ball around the course the best way you know how. How many times have you seen a fellow competitor hit poor tee shots and then make absolutely great recovery shots time after time – and all you hear is him complaining about the tee shots. The individual shots do not show up on the card, unless you allow them to through a poor attitude.

'Ego point': I'm convinced that in every round of tournament golf there is what I like to call an ego point, a turning point which determines the final result of the complete round. I can remember a Pro-Am in Chattanooga a few years ago, when after eight horrible holes in which I had failed to hit but one in regulation, I was faced with an eight-foot putt for par. I took great care with it and made it, for some unknown reason. At the conclusion of the 18 holes I had recorded a 66, six under par. I'm convinced, had I missed that particular putt at that time, I would have recorded a 74 or 75. Make an extra effort after the 'turning point' comes. It will normally mean far more than just the one immediate stroke.

Gamble: How many times do we fail to know our limitations and waste strokes because of senseless gambling? It's useless to gamble unless the odds are in our favour. If we gambled on the horses like we do on some golf shots with the odds we have, we would all be on welfare. Control your compulsions and do what the situation calls for. We cannot solve all problems with first one solution. I'm convinced that Billy Joe Patton lost the 1956 US Masters because he was too bold on the fourth round. By the same token Billy Casper probably lost the same title in 1969 by playing too safe on the fourth and final day. Had each changed his tactics at the proper time and did what the situation called for, each may easily have won in those respective years.

Nothing says you have to hit toward the flag every time. What's really wrong with the middle of the green? Play 'scared' on occasions by dodging the out-of-bounds lakes and high rough and let the gallery think what it wants. Take pride in your total score, not just great shots performed on the course which never reach the scoring columns.

Tour v club professionals: Since the club professional lacks the opportunity to practise and play as the touring professional he must suffer the fact that in each round of golf he plays he will lose two strokes while the touring pro is saving two. That is a lot of difference in 18 holes of golf. Make up your mind when you start out that you are going to save at least two shots. Make an opportunity out of every missed shot to save a shot. For example, if on the first hole you get in trouble, when you get in trouble on the second say to yourself, 'This is an opportunity already for me to save a shot. If I continue to play like this I may save four or five shots during this round.'

Make golf a game within a game. It's much more fun for you and your companions. Have you ever watched a noted scrambler when he misses a green? He thrives on this, knowing all along he's going to get up and down and save a shot – and make you mad. He enjoys getting up and down and at times seems to enjoy getting into trouble. He has made a 'game' out of the challenges to improve his scrambling.

Carelessness: The less we play the more careless shots we hit. This comes from playing at home with the members, becoming lax in technique and being satisfied to shoot a certain score, just enough to win by. We need some type of goal in front of us. Learn to hit careful shots, because carelessness becomes a habit hard to break. Each year I always try to break the course record at my club. This is when I score my best. During the rest of the season I'm content to score a satisfactory round, because I have no goal. But without a goal we become careless.

The law of probability: Have you ever thought what the odds are on making a six to eight-foot putt? Fifty per cent would be extremely high, yet in a tournament we get upset because we miss one of this length. It doesn't make sense, and yet because of this type of attitude our scores increase. We have the wrong attitude. We must learn to be patient and accept the odds. Realizing the odds makes for a more positive attitude and a lower final score.

Experimenting: As club professionals we learn too many ways of hitting the ball and develop fair ability in several ways, but seldom excellent in any. Stay with your tournament stroke, for here lies your major ability. We teach different methods to get the subject across to our students, but this is one time we don't practise what we teach. Stay with one method – the method that you use in competition which will produce for you the lowest score.

Personal records: When you're hitting a certain shot well, make a note of why – how you feel, what you are thinking about during execution, and so on. We tend to forget quickly. Without records we can be disillusioned, which will affect our attitude. What we think is wrong may not be the problem at all if the facts were known. We then develop a mental problem which is not a problem at all. Many times we think we're putting badly, but by looking at the record we see that the footage of putts is the problem and it can be poor chipping and not hitting greens in regulation rather than the actual putting.

All professionals like Hubie Smith and professional organizations are constantly searching for ways and means of playing better golf, not only for themselves but also for every golfer and would-be golfer. But I doubt if the time will ever come when there will be nothing left to learn. If it does, then the game must inevitably go into decline. As a professional of very long standing, certainly as a teaching professional, I'm still constantly learning, very often from the most unlikely sources, such as my own pupils. And I shall expect to go on learning as long as I teach and play golf. I don't mean accepting all and every opinion; as I've stated before, I'm only interested in facts.

The *new* psychology is fascinating. Its depths can surely not be plumbed, even by a qualified doctor. I don't believe that there should be too much delving without qualified medical assistance. Hubie Smith went as far as the pros need to go within the bounds of common sense; no amount of psychology can be substituted for physical skill and the work it demands. Nevertheless, its importance should not be ignored. It might be that many a frustrated golfer will come away from the psychiatrist's couch a much better player, having been cured of the inhibitions which blocked progress.

But you can take that progress even further by adopting a professional approach – and approaching a professional.

CHAPTER FOURTEEN

A NEW WAY OF LEARNING

In my view Swedes are an intelligent people, far-sighted and wonderful innovators. They're not afraid of hearing other points of view and, when necessary, soliciting advice from whatever source they feel would benefit them. In the sphere of golf they've gone to great lengths in inviting Americans and British 'known' teachers to lecture their professionals.

Gunnar Mueller was for years the leading Swedish tour player. Now, partially retired from the tour, he's a successful club pro and teacher at the attractive Lillevik club on the shores of the Baltic, a few miles north of a beautiful fishing town called Simrishamn. Gunnar is a master of the art of improvization, and in particular at devizing exercises to help players improve their game.

I'll never forget the miniature nine-hole pitch and putt course he made in the quite small garden (back and front) of the cottage he'd rented in Canterbury during the Open at nearby Sandwich. It certainly taxed the skill of a number of pros who were staying with him and others who visited during that week. It wound around trees and over hedges, paths, lawns and flower-beds; short but diabolically cunning. I doubt if Lee Trevino could have equalled the par of 27.

With his kind permission the following pages are adapted from his *Swedish PGA Manual of Golf Training* – for 'enthusiasts and those with a desire to learn'.

The complete manual is available for anyone who cares to write to Gunnar at the Osterlens Golf Klubb, Lillevik, Simrishamn 27200, Sweden; although, as he says, the manual is never finished and he is continuously adding to it as he thinks up new ideas and picks up a few old ones along the way.

---

1. PRACTICE GROUND – ADDRESS ROUTINE

Equipment:	*club and practice balls.*
What you will improve:	*preparation.*
Number training: (group size)	*8. Tee up a ball and choose a target.*

Position yourself about three yards behind the ball and select a mark in front of the ball that lies directly on the line of the target.

Take up a position one to two yards distance from the ball at right angles to the target line. Grip the club.

Walk up to the ball and set the clubface towards your spot. Take your stance after setting the clubhead.

---

2. Practice ground – Weight-shift drill

Equipment:	*club, balls, tees.*
What you will improve:	*correct weight transference and rhythm.*
Number training:	*1 to 4 at a time.*

Tee up the balls in a straight line about eight inches apart at right angles to the target line. The player will hit all the balls walking in perpetual motion one after another. The right foot is planted firmly for the wide backswing and then the left foot is planted for a wide follow-through swing. It looks like a duck's walk. Keep in rhythm.

Swing back from the top of the follow through and step on to the right foot.

3. PRACTICE GROUND – COIN DRILL

Equipment: *club, small coin, balls.*
What you will improve: *grip firmness and the path of the swing.*
Number training: *8.*

a) Grip the club with your left hand. With your right hand place a coin [5p piece] between the pad of your left palm and the top of the grip opposite the little finger. The coin then comes directly above the side of the grip. Grip with both hands and hold the coin in place through the whole swing. Hit a few balls still securing the coin.

b) Take the left hand grip again. Place the coin on the second joint of the left thumb. Now, grip with your right hand. Keep the coin in place throughout the whole swing. Hit a couple of shots with the same intention.

c) Take your grip with both hands and let a fellow student wedge the coin between the right thumb and the base of the right index finger. You can do this yourself by gripping with both hands then, removing the left hand from the club, inserting the coin and regripping with the left hand. Hit a few shots and feel a lot of control.

3(a). *To cure a slice.*

Place the coin an inch in front of the ball, slightly to the right of the target line, and try to hit the ball and the coin.

3(b). *To make a good follow through.*

Place the coin four inches in front of the ball, directly on the target line. Try to hit the ball and the coin. The object is not to hit the coin but to try.

4. PRACTICE GROUND – ARMSWING EXERCISE

Equipment:	*club, balls, chairs.*
What you will improve:	*feeling the club and ball.*
Number training:	*8.*

In fact use stools instead of chairs if you can. Sit on the front right side of the chair. Fold in your right leg along the side of the chair. Tee the balls up and hit them with the strength of your hands and arms.

5. GOLF COURSE – CONCENTRATION

Equipment:	*set of clubs and balls.*
What you will improve:	*mental stamina.*
Number training:	*'X' number of 3 balls.*

Hit your driving range balls, pretending you are playing round the course. Continue with your imaginary second shot and so on. Skip the chipping and putting. When you've played the 18 holes in your imagination you'll have an approximate idea of what you would have scored. Now to the main task.

On the course: you'll start concentrating on the shot you're about to play, 30 seconds before impact. Do your best. After the shot you relax until you have 30 seconds to go before your next shot. Like a chess player does after his move, turn off the clock and relax. If you've played badly, you should rest a little after play, then analyse and go to the practice ground to make the correction.

6. PRACTICE GROUND – LEFT-HAND SHOTS FOR RIGHT-HAND PLAYERS. THE REVERSE APPLIES FOR LEFT-HAND PLAYERS

Equipment: *9-iron and ball.*
What you will
  improve: *versatility.*
Number training: *8.*

Turn a 9-iron so that the toe is grounded and facing opposite the normal direction. Stand on the other side of the ball. Hold the left hand below the right. It's just the reverse of normal play. On the course when you find your ball near the 'wrong' side of a tree trunk it's useful to be able to play this kind of shot. If the ball is nearer to the trunk than 5cm or so, it may need a putter-type shot.

7. PRACTICE GROUND – SHORT GAME/HIGH PITCHES

Equipment: *High jump posts, net, 2in × 4in piece of wood.*
What you will improve: *finesse shots, the toughest ones.*
Number training: *maximum of 3.*

Mark out a teeing ground. Put the high jump net in front of it. Limit the target zone with the piece of wood. The ball must carry the net but stop before it hits the wood.

Indoors you can use gym mats and nets to stop the balls.

8. PRACTICE GROUND – WATER SHOTS

Equipment: *short iron, puddles of water.*
What you will improve: *judgment about possible shots.*
Number training: *small group.*

This is essentially a warm weather drill. Make a target area 15-30 yards from the puddles. Put on your rain clothes and take off your shoes and socks. Take your stance carefully so you don't move the ball. Play the shot as you would a buried lie in a bunker. Try three different situations:

1. The ball halfway above the surface.
2. The upper part of ball touching the surface.
3. The ball a full inch below the surface.

Don't ground the club.

Remember that you have a free drop from casual water through the green and even in a bunker. But you must find a dry spot within the bunker not nearer the hole.

---

9. PRACTICE GROUND – DIFFERENT BALL CONTACTS

Equipment:	*clubs and driving range balls.*
What you will improve:	*awareness of where the clubhead is throughout the swing.*
Number training:	*8.*

a) Put two balls near to each other, but not touching. Try to hit both with one swing. At best, the result is a hook and slice. Tee the balls up if you wish.

b) Try to hit a topped shot with a full swing. The best ones might get the ball to roll only a couple of metres. Try this also with a wood and a teed up ball.

c) Tee the ball up. Use a fairway wood or a long iron. Try to hit a low clean shot from the teed up lie.

---

10. BUNKER – BASIC SHOT WITH UMBRELLA

Equipment:	*sand-wedge, balls and umbrella.*
What you will improve:	*target practice to bigger and easier target.*
Number training:	*a few players simultaneously in a bunker.*

Open up the umbrella and put it into the ground (one for each player). Try to explode from the bunker into the umbrella. Makes a good competition.

11. BUNKER – BASIC SHOT WITH A BOARD

Equipment:	*sand-wedge, balls and board.*
What you will improve:	*the 'bounce' effect.*
Number training:	*as many as the bunker will hold comfortably up to three or four.*

Put the board into the bunker so that it's just covered with sand, and put the ball on top. Then play the ball out of the bunker.

12. PRACTICE GROUND – CHIP AND PITCH

Equipment:	*bags, tyres, club and balls.*
What you will improve:	*short game.*
Number training:	*8*

Put the bag between you and the tyre. Try to chip the ball into the tyre. Use different clubs if you want to be a real champion.

13. PITCHING GREEN – SLALOM CHIPPING

Equipment:	*pitching wedge, balls, posts for gates.*
What you will improve:	*to have fun when you practice.*
Number training:	*maximum of 4.*

Arrange a slalom track that ends with a green and a hole. Play through all the gates with your chips and hole out in as few strokes as possible.

Use the putter only on the green.

14. BUNKER – BASIC SHOT WITH TEES

Equipment:	*balls, sand-wedge, tees.*
What you will improve:	*smooth swinging.*
Number training:	*a few in the bunker at the same time.*

Tee the ball up in the bunker but keep the tee totally hidden in the sand. Try to break the tee during the swing.

15. Practice putting green – Putting

Equipment:	*putter, balls and tees.*
What you will improve:	*how a borrow on the green effects the ball at different speeds.*
Number training:	*pairs.*

On a long putt, line the tees along the line you think will be right. Then putt and check how well you anticipated the break.

Make a funnel through which the ball must pass to reach the hole. Make it two feet deep and let your line to the hole be in the centre. Now, try a few putts.

16. Practice ground – 'On your knees'

Equipment:	*clubs, balls, mat or towel.*
What you will improve:	*inventiveness from trouble.*
Number training:	*4.*

Kneel on the towel and try to hit the ball as far as possible. Check which club gives you the best result. Start with the balls teed up. To succeed you must use a very flat swing plane. You're imitating a lie on the course where the ball is under a tree or a bush.

ANATOMY OF THE SWING

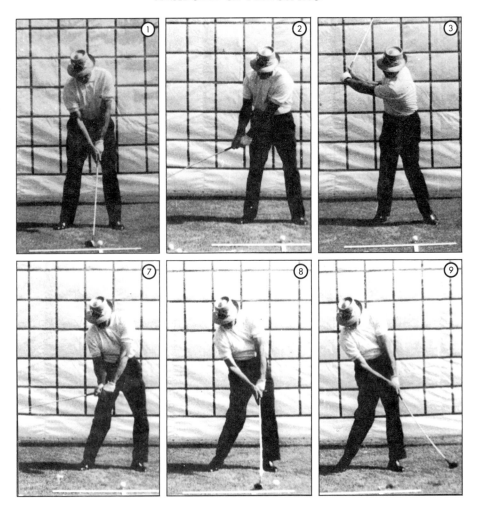

The following 8 pages analyse 12 stages in the swings of four superstars. The figures refer to the number of the photograph in each sequence.

1. The assembly is as much as 60% of the swing in terms of getting it all right. Note their firm stance, with even pressure between legs and feet. Sam Snead's wide stance and the faint inside curve of his knees allows not only the player to grip the ground but also the ground to grip the player. Sam is just pulling the clubhead away from the ball and the slight bowing of the shaft is the effect of inertia in the clubhead. It doesn't want to move. Bruce Crampton's hips are a little open and he has his head tilted to the right in the Nicklaus fashion. Tommy Aaron shows all the same qualities as

SAM SNEAD

his fellow-American Snead, but it's perhaps even more obvious that his knees
are 'drawn in' to give him a secure base. Like Snead, he looks into the back
of the ball, while Gary Player looks directly at it.

With his right knee 'kick-start' Player has (to use golfing jargon) a
'weaker' left-hand grip than the others, but the disposition of the left hand is
variable. Here it's twined round a fraction more to the left than his
colleagues, but his right-hand grip is well triggered. The thumb and
forefinger are set 'on top' of the grip in the position to which it will return
through contact. Both Snead and Aaron have well-triggered right thumb
and forefinger firmly closed, while Crampton holds his right-hand trigger
rather more to the right of his shaft or grip centre.

ANATOMY OF THE SWING

2-3. All four players have extended away from centre, with Player perhaps the most pronounced: they don't simply slide along with their arms to the right. The shoulders coil round to the right on the hip platform and in each case the right leg supports this coil and holds the body into the centre. This winding of the upper body against the lower with the pillar of the right leg tilted into centre doesn't exclude hip turn, but it does initiate a responsive force which reacts when the swing changes direction. Nor do these players tilt to the left; indeed there is virtually no change of the even pressure adopted at assembly.

The wrist angle collection adduction has begun with all four of them in

BRUCE CRAMPTON

picture 3. At this stage Snead has more than Aaron, who has more than Player, who has more than Crampton, and yet . . .

4. . . . at the top of the backswing it's Aaron who has collected most wrist angle, followed by Snead, Player and Crampton. It matters little: these differences are simply governed by (and well within) the physical and psychological tolerances of each player. All have kept the back of the left hand and wrist in place for a neutral clubface position.
Crampton displays no elevation of the left heel. Aaron has just a touch, perhaps, and Player too, while Snead has easily the most at about an inch.

ANATOMY OF THE SWING

5. *In all cases the lower body has been the first area to respond to the directional change of the swing. The left heel is now firmly planted and initiates the wind up of the left side in support of the contact. The hips have moved back square to the target line and the shoulders have shed 45° of their right-angle at the top of the backswing.*

All four players have retained their wrist angle. In fact Crampton has 'gained' a little more and his right knee and heel are moving up towards his left knee and heel respectively. Snead and Aaron are 'on their way', but as yet Snead has not caught up with his younger colleagues. All four players could justifiably be described as having upright planes.

TOMMY AARON

6-10. The right elbow is close into the right side of the forward swing, while the right knee has progressed to the left. Both Crampton and Player have raised the right heel well to the left, but by contact all four have become elevated. Wrist angles are retained, and their hands lead the clubhead into contact. All are well centred by the rightward orientation of face to ball; all left-arm radii are intact; all the left legs are winding up.

Note the common factor of the abducted left hand and wrist – abducted from the swing centre. The arching of the left wrist caused by centrifugal force is seen clearly. The square clubface is held tightly into the back of the ball but after contact the clubface begins to turn gradually leftwards.

ANATOMY OF THE SWING

The progressive bowing of the right knee, the right heel lift, the sustained head centering and the winding left leg (to straight) has set the body spinning from hips to shoulders round the vertical axis (the spine) as the arms are 'flung' away in orbit round it. Force overcomes resistance as their arms cross over and the club crosses a line parallel to the target line. The hands and wrists are still abducted.

11-12. Although quite late – and it should be – the rotation of the head serves to provide a secondary 'hub' to keep the swing flowing. Notice the upward spiralling of the body in the final phase of the four swings. There's not even lip service paid to the notion of 'keeping down'. Balance is perfect

GARY PLAYER

*in each case, now organized by the completely coiled left side from foot to
shoulder (that area now contains all the bodyweight), supported by the right
knee curve and culminating as it touches the left knee. The hands are high
and the arms have gracefully 'maypoled' as the kinetic energy finally runs
out. The hands and wrists are once more adducted to swing centre. You'll
notice from the squared background to Sam Snead that throughout the
course of the entire swing his head has hardly moved from its position of
assembly. The same would be true of the other three.*

*It's well within you to cultivate, within your tolerances, a golf swing that
contains all these star qualities. There's only one swing to learn.*

INDEX